Wisconsin

Wisconsin

Jean F. Blashfield

Children's Press®
A Division of Grolier Publishing
New York London Hong Kong Sydney
Danbury, Connecticut

Frontispiece: A rural dairy farm
Front cover: Autumn colors near Gleason, Wisconsin
Back cover: Sunrise over Lake Michigan, Milwaukee

Consultant: Jane M. Pederson, Professor, University of Wisconsin—Eau Claire

Please note: All statistics are as up-to-date as possible at the time of publication.

Visit Children's Press on the Internet at http://publishing.grolier.com

Book production by Editorial Directions, Inc.

Library of Congress Cataloging-in-Publication Data

Blashfield, Jean F.
    Wisconsin / by Jean F. Blashfield.
      p. cm. — (America the beautiful. Second series)
    Includes bibliographical references (p.) and index.
    Summary: A brief introduction to the geography, history, natural resources,
industries, cities, and people of Wisconsin.
    ISBN 0-516-20640-0
    1. Wisconsin—Juvenile literature. [1. Wisconsin.] I. Title. II. Series.
F581.3.8568 1998
977.5—dc21   97-40706
                                                                          CIP
                                                                          AC

This book is for Etta Gray,

who has made life in Wisconsin

so pleasant for me.

Rural church

Holstein cows

Milwaukee skyline

Contents

Eric Heiden

Port of Milwaukee worker

Mississippi River valley

Cheese production

Carrie Chapman Catt

CHAPTER ONE

Defining
a State

Wisconsin is a mixture of wilderness and city, farming and manufacturing, gentle prairie and tumbled cliffs, progressive politics and hidebound tradition. It is a state defined by people from many different lands, all of whom have added their own traditions to Wisconsin's rich cultural heritage.

It is also a state defined by water. All but the southern border with Illinois and about 100 miles (160 km) of the border with Minnesota and northern Michigan were defined by nature, in the form of rivers, rather than by politicians.

It is a state defined by ice. Wisconsin is about the same size as neighboring Iowa, but it has a greater variety of landscapes because it once was covered by a glacier, a great ice sheet that gouged and transformed the land as it retreated.

Wisconsin is a state defined by cows. Known as "America's Dairyland," Wisconsin produces milk, cream, butter, and more cheese than any other state. Wisconsinites take pride in the humorous nickname "Cheesehead."

In 1881, restaurant-owner Edward Berner of Two Rivers concocted a dessert that he would sell only on Sundays. It consisted of ice cream with chocolate sauce, and it became known as the sundae—with an "e," not a "y." Trust a Wisconsinite to make sure that the new treat was made with cream.

Canoeing on Whishow Lake in the Wisconsin Northwoods

Opposite: Wisconsin immigrants built churches and practiced their religion and traditions in their new home.

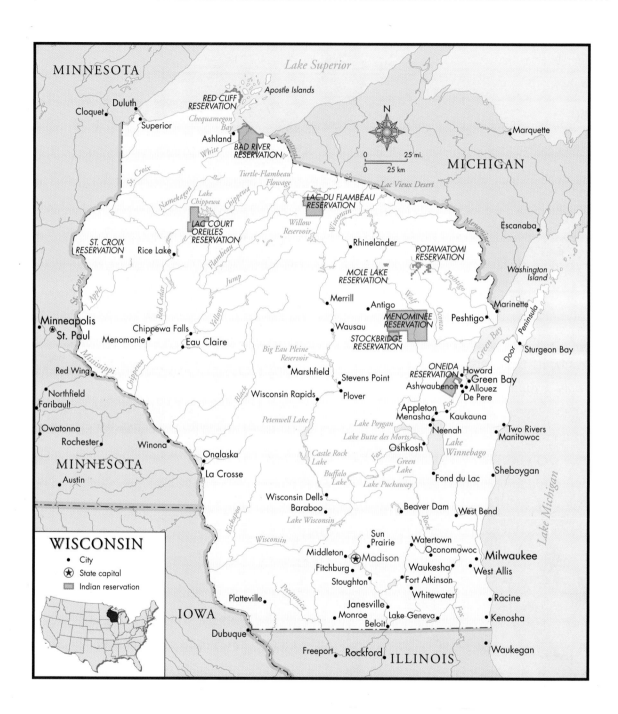

MINNESOTA

Lake Superior

RED CLIFF
RESERVATION

Apostle Islands

Cloquet
Duluth

Superior

Chequamegon
Bay

Ashland

White

BAD RIVER
RESERVATION

Montreal

Marquette

Lac Vieux Desert

MICHIGAN

N

0   25 mi.
0   25 km

St. Croix

Namekagon

Turtle-Flambeau
Flowage

Lake
Chippewa

Chippewa

LAC DU FLAMBEAU
RESERVATION

Menominee

Escanaba

ST. CROIX
RESERVATION

Rice Lake

LAC COURT
OREILLES
RESERVATION

Willow
Reservoir

Wisconsin

Rhinelander

POTAWATOMI
RESERVATION

Washington
Island

Flambeau

Red Cedar

Jump

Yellow

MOLE LAKE
RESERVATION

Peshtigo

Wolf

Oconto

Marinette

Peshtigo

Door
Peninsula

Merrill

Antigo

Minneapolis
St. Paul

Chippewa Falls

Menomonie

Eau Claire

Big Eau Pleine
Reservoir

Wausau

MENOMINEE
RESERVATION

STOCKBRIDGE
RESERVATION

Green Bay

Sturgeon Bay

Red Wing

Chippewa

Marshfield

Stevens Point

ONEIDA
RESERVATION

Howard

Green Bay

Ashwaubenon

Allouez

Northfield
Faribault

Black

Wisconsin Rapids

Plover

De Pere

Fox

Appleton

Menasha

Kaukauna

Owatonna

Rochester

Winona

Petenwell Lake

Lake Poygan

Lake Butte des Morts

Neenah

Lake
Winnebago

Two Rivers

Manitowoc

Onalaska

MINNESOTA

La Crosse

Castle Rock
Lake

Fox

Oshkosh

Green
Lake

Sheboygan

Austin

Buffalo
Lake

Lake Puckaway

Fond du Lac

Kickapoo

Wisconsin Dells

Baraboo

Lake Wisconsin

Beaver Dam

West Bend

Lake Michigan

Wisconsin

Sun
Prairie

Watertown

Oconomowoc

Milwaukee

Middleton

Madison

Waukesha

West Allis

Fitchburg

Rock

Fort Atkinson

Stoughton

Whitewater

Racine

Platteville

Pecatonica

Janesville

Monroe

Lake Geneva

Fox

Kenosha

Beloit

IOWA

Dubuque

Freeport

Rockford

ILLINOIS

Waukegan

WISCONSIN

• City

⊛ State capital

▨ Indian reservation

10 WISCONSIN

As missionaries traveled down the great river that runs through the heart of the land that would one day become the thirtieth state, they asked the Native Americans the river's name. One heard it as "Meskousing." Another listened more closely and imitated the sound he heard as "Ouisconsin," which became "Wisconsin." The name is generally accepted to mean "gathering of the waters." ■

Wisconsin is also called the "Badger State" because many of the miners who opened up the state in the southwest were so busy digging for lead that they didn't have time to build houses. Instead, they burrowed into the ground like badgers to rest at night. The mascot of the justly famous University of Wisconsin is called Bucky Badger.

Wisconsin's state motto is "Forward." Throughout Wisconsin's history, the people of this state have helped lead the United States into the future.

Opposite: Geopolitical map of Wisconsin

CHAPTER TWO

The Making of a State

Life came to Wisconsin only when the glaciers that covered North America four times over the last million years retreated to the north. Plants and animals from the south moved into the once-frozen land as the glacier retreated. Humans came, too.

Little is known about those first people, small bands of hunters called Paleo-Indians who arrived about 11,000 B.C. The only evidence of their existence is the stone tools they used to hunt and scrape hides. Once called arrowheads, these tools are now called stone points. Scientists now know that bows and arrows were not used in Wisconsin until much later.

Native American burial mounds, Aztalan State Park

As the climate became warmer during the Archaic Period (7000 B.C.), people inhabited Wisconsin for longer periods. Some of these people began to use metallic copper, which was found around Lake Superior. The remnants of ancient mines and fires in which the metal was melted have been found by Green Bay and along the Fox River.

The Archaic people gradually evolved into the Woodland people, who gardened and made pottery. Much of what we know about the people of this period came from the mounds they left behind.

During the period from 200 B.C. to A.D. 500, the Hopewell people lived in the southwestern part of the state, along the fertile rivers. These people were farmers, but they also made artis-

Opposite: Autumn on Lake Otter near Tomahawk

Effigy Mounds

During the Late Woodland Period, many native groups built mounds in the shape of animals. Called effigy mounds, they were about 36 inches (90 cm) high. They may have marked the boundaries of an individual group's territory, or perhaps the center of a territory to which smaller bands returned once a year. The makers of these mounds were probably the ancestors of the Winnebago, or Ho-Chunk, Indians.

Wisconsin had more effigy mounds than any other state. Unfortunately, most of them have been destroyed. Those that survive are located in state parks, such as Lizard Mounds near West Bend, Kegonza State Park near Stoughton, and Devil's Lake State Park at Baraboo.

Another form of effigy mound is similar to a mirror image—dug into the soil instead of built up. Called an *intaglio*, the only surviving effigy of this type is a panther, located in Fort Atkinson. ■

tic ceremonial pottery. The copper that they found and traded in Wisconsin ended up in areas of the country as far away as Florida.

The Hopewell culture was gradually replaced by the Mississippian, during which agriculture became firmly established. In Wisconsin, archaeologists find evidence of this period—from A.D. 1100 to 1300—at Aztalan State Park, on the Crawfish River near Lake Mills. The people of the Hopewell culture built villages complete with houses and pyramid-shaped ceremonial mounds inside stockades (high fences). The Mississippian people were probably the first people in Wisconsin to use bows and arrows for hunting.

Gradually, through the Midwest, the people of the Mississippian culture began to split up into separate tribes. It was these tribes who met the European explorers.

In the 1800s, pioneers settled at Aztalan.

Indians of Written History

The Winnebago, or Ho-Chunk, occupied most of Wisconsin until the Ojibwa (called the Chippewa by the French) moved in from Canada. Attacking Iroquois forced the Ojibwa to move west, where they tried to take Winnebago land. This struggle continued for the better part of 200 years.

By 1616, because of the Europeans' eagerness to trade for beaver furs, the Ottawa and Huron of the Northeast established trading centers by Chequamegon Bay at the western end of Lake Superior. They, too, fought the local Winnebago, almost destroying them.

Other Native American tribes in Wisconsin at the time included the Ojibwa in the North Woods. The Menominee occupied a large territory near Green Bay. These groups spoke languages in what is called the Algonquin family, as did the smaller tribes called the Miami (at the southern end of Lake Michigan) and the Fox (near Green Bay). In the western part of the area were the Dakota Sioux (also called Santee). They moved west in the 1700s. The scattered Winnebago also spoke a Siouan language, but their lifestyle was more like that of the Algonquin tribes.

The Coming Europeans

In 1634, while searching for a route to the Pacific Ocean, the French explorer Jean Nicolet traveled by canoe through the Straits of Mackinac, becoming the first European to enter Lake Michigan. Following the western shore, he and his men entered Green Bay. They finally stepped ashore at the location that later became the city of Green Bay.

In about 1660, René Ménard, a Roman Catholic priest, opened a mission on the Chippewa River to convert Huron Indians. When the Huron moved away, Ménard tried to follow and was never heard from again. About five years later, Father Claude Allouez established several missions, including one on the present-day site of De Pere.

The first settler's house in Wisconsin was built on the spot where the city of Green Bay now stands. Pierre Esprit Radisson

Today, Ojibwa gather annually at the Bad River Reservation to celebrate the traditional harvest festival.

French explorer
Jean Nicolet lands in
Wisconsin.

from Canada, exploring with his brother-in-law Médart Chouart de Groseilliers, built a log house inside a stockade on the bay.

The Native Americans had been fighting among themselves over who had the right to trade furs with the Europeans. Nicolas Perrot, who was well known to the tribes, was determined to break the hold that the Ottawa had on the fur trade. In 1671, he went to the Algonquin tribes who lived along the Mississippi and persuaded them to give their allegiance to France. In 1685, he became French governor of the region.

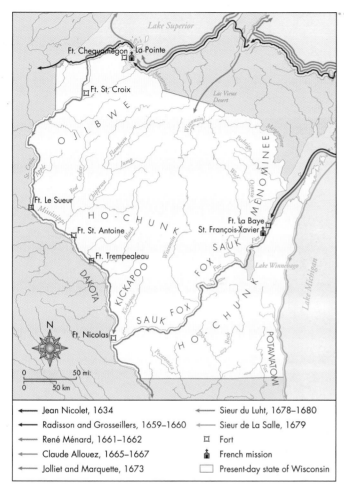

Exploration of Wisconsin

Map legend:
- ← Jean Nicolet, 1634
- ← Radisson and Grosseillers, 1659–1660
- ← René Ménard, 1661–1662
- ← Claude Allouez, 1665–1667
- ← Jolliet and Marquette, 1673
- ← Sieur du Luht, 1678–1680
- ← Sieur de La Salle, 1679
- ⌑ Fort
- ⛪ French mission
- ▭ Present-day state of Wisconsin

Marquette and Jolliet

Count Frontenac, governor of New France, or Canada, for King Louis XIV of France, sent seven men southward on a mission to explore the heart of the Americas. Frontenac wanted to claim as much land as possible to prevent it from falling into the hands of the Spanish, who were known to be moving northward from the Gulf of Mexico.

The seven men included a fur trader, Louis Jolliet, and a missionary priest, Père (Father) Jacques Marquette. The remaining five men were boatmen, called voyageurs, hired by fur companies to transport furs and supplies. The small group paddled

their canoes into Green Bay, past the mission that had already been established at De Pere, and into the Fox River.

The Mascouten Indian village at present-day Berlin was as far as Europeans had previously gone. Two Miami Indians reluctantly agreed to guide the seven explorers to a place where they could carry their canoes overland to a bigger river. On June 14, 1673, the two guides helped the explorers carry their goods "2,700 paces" (about 2 miles, or 3.2 km) to another, wider river. As the seven explorers paddled down the Wisconsin River, their Miami guides, eager to avoid the Winnebago Indians who lived along the river, quickly returned to their village.

Wide-eyed, Marquette and Jolliet traveled down the Wisconsin River for seven days, until they reached the vast Mississippi River. Stunned by its size, they bravely paddled downstream until they became afraid that they would run into the Spanish. All that remains of their adventure is a copy of Father Marquette's journal, which he had left behind at the De Pere mission.

Opposite: Marquette and Jolliet traveling with voyageur guides

Charles de Langlade fought in the French and Indian War before settling in Wisconsin.

The Fur Trade and New Ownership

For the next 100 years, Europeans continued to regard Wisconsin only as a source of furs. For many Native Americans, though, it became a refuge.

The Iroquois from eastern Canada and New England moved westward, fighting other Native Americans to take over additional fur territory. The Iroquois pushed the Ottawa from Canada and the Potawatomi from Michigan past Lakes Michigan and Superior into Wisconsin. The Sauk also moved in from Michigan and gradually merged with the Fox Indians. The Ojibwa, or Chippewa, benefited most from the European demand for furs.

In 1745, Charles de Langlade became Wisconsin's first permanent European settler. Langlade, who had an Ottawa mother and French father, moved to the Green Bay area, where he built the first farm in the upper Midwest. Langlade was adept at military strategy and fought on the side of the French in the French and Indian War (1754–1763). Langlade was later called the "father of Wisconsin" because he was the most prominent of the few fur traders who settled there before 1820.

In 1763, the French lost control of the area, including Wisconsin, in the French and Indian War. The treaty they signed gave huge territories of North America to Great Britain.

Most of the fighting in the American Revolution (1775–1783) took place far to the east of Wisconsin, and the few traders in Wisconsin who knew anything about it sided with the British. When the war was over, the huge region called the Northwest Territories—between the Ohio River and the Mississippi River—was granted to the new United States. No one came to relieve the British of the area, though, so a few British soldiers continued to control Wisconsin land until the War of 1812.

Getting Ready for Settlement

Starting in 1800, Wisconsin was briefly a county (called St. Claire) in the Indiana Territory. Forts were built at Green Bay and Prairie du Chien.

Using his influence in Washington, D.C., businessman John Jacob Astor managed to wrest the Upper Mississippi fur trade from the British and French. By the 1820s, though, fur traders had already hunted and trapped nearly all the wildlife in this part of the country. The fur trade was in decline. Settlers who wanted to farm the fertile land were eyeing Wisconsin, which was then part of Illinois Territory. These settlers were eager to force the Native Americans off the land.

In 1825, the U.S. government took its first steps toward seizing the Wisconsin land. By signing the Treaty of Prairie du Chien, several tribes agreed to establish boundaries to the land they claimed as their own. They did not realize that this step would

An early fur trader checks his traps.

eventually cause them to lose their land. Two years later, members of the Winnebago tribe, led by a man named Red Bird, killed several settlers at Prairie du Chien. Government retribution caused the Winnebago to rise, and the so-called Winnebago War was prevented only by Red Bird's surrender. The region, which had a major supply of lead ore underground, was ceded to the U.S. government, and settlement began.

Lead Mining

The fur trade dwindled, but Wisconsin had the good fortune to have lead ore in the southwestern part of the territory. The prospect of lucrative mines brought many miners up the Mississippi to settle. In later years, the easily opened surface mines ran out. Miners from Cornwall, England, then moved in, bringing with them the technical knowledge necessary to mine metals from deep in the earth.

Henry Dodge was prominent among the lead miners. Although the U.S. government had decreed in an 1816 treaty that the Winnebago Indians owned the rights to much of the lead-mining land, Dodge and his followers settled in and refused to move. The government then forced the Winnebago to accept several new treaties between 1829 and 1833, and the Winnebago lost their rights to the lead region.

In 1832, Black Hawk, a warrior of the combined Fox and Sauk tribe that had been forced into Iowa, gathered disgruntled Native Americans around him. The government refused to let them return to Illinois to hunt and grow corn. Black Hawk led about 1,000 men, women, and children back into Illinois. He soon realized that he could not prevail and was heading back toward Iowa when he ran into a militia unit that ignored the white flag his people were carrying. They attacked, and Black Hawk was forced to fight back. The terrified militiamen ran away. The equally terrified Indians fled up the Rock River into Wisconsin. They tried to hide, but settlers such as Henry Dodge wanted to eliminate the Native American presence entirely and pursued them.

Weeks later, the starving remnants of Black Hawk's band were pushed into a final battle at the mouth of the Bad Axe River on the Mississippi, about 40 miles (64 km) north of the Wisconsin. When the battle was over, all but 100 to 150 of the Native Americans had been killed. Black Hawk himself was imprisoned. The savage and brutal reaction of the whites discouraged other Indians from trying to go home again.

Chief Black Hawk

African-Americans

African-Americans were among the early trappers and traders in Wisconsin. Several worked as traders in the northern part of the territory, around Marinette, soon after the American Revolution.

Today, African-Americans are trying to recover their heritage, destroyed by slave traders centuries ago.

African-American settlers began farming the land by 1793. Several towns were founded by African-American people.

At the same time, despite territorial laws that forbade slavery, a number of black slaves were also living in Wisconsin. They were owned by Southerners who had moved into the territory. In fact, Henry Dodge owned slaves until 1838.

Becoming a State

The new U. S. government created the Northwest Territories out of the Upper Midwest region that was taken from the British in the American Revolution. A territory had to have a population of 60,000 to qualify for statehood. It didn't take long for Wisconsin to reach that number. In 1825, the Erie Canal in New York was opened, and it became possible for settlers from the East to go all the way to Chicago by boat. Many decided to settle in Wisconsin, and a government land office was opened at Mineral Point.

Between 1840 and 1850, thousands of settlers arrived from New England. Among them were James Doty, a New Yorker who founded Madison and became the second territorial governor, and Nelson Dewey of Connecticut, who became the first governor of the state of Wisconsin.

As its population grew, Wisconsin was part of Indiana Territory, then part of Illinois, and finally part of Michigan. In 1836, Wisconsin became a separate territory that included Iowa, Minnesota, and the eastern part of the Dakotas. The region that eventually became the state of Wisconsin had about 11,000 inhabitants. Henry Dodge was named territorial governor. The first territorial legislature met in the small southwestern town of Belmont. Only nine years later, Wisconsin had the 60,000 residents required for statehood. In fact, Wisconsin grew faster than any other state, with more than 300,000 people by 1850.

The people in the territory had to approve a state constitution before statehood could be granted, but they rejected Wisconsin's first attempt because it outlawed banks. Businessmen knew that banks would be important to a developing state. They demanded—and received—a revised constitution, leaving the question of banks unresolved. Wisconsin became the thirtieth state on May 29, 1848.

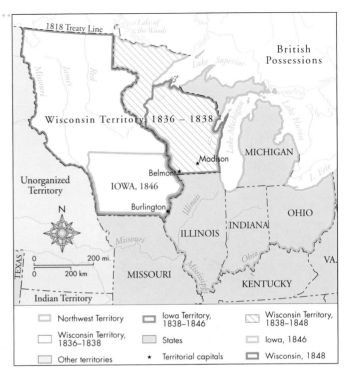

Historical map of Wisconsin

Nelson Dewey State Park

CHAPTER THREE

Growing into the Modern World

German emigrants embark at Hamburg for a new life in the United States.

When it became a state, Wisconsin was populated by three groups. The first group was made up of people who were born in Wisconsin or had moved there from surrounding states. They were often the settlers who cleared the land for farms.

The second group came through the Erie Canal from the East. These people already knew how a new state functioned, and they came prepared to buy large amounts of land to develop into towns and villages.

The third group was made up of immigrants from Europe. At that time, countries in Europe were experiencing rapid population growth and many of them had more people than land or jobs. Discovering that there was no way for them to earn a good living, people with a taste for adventure began to look to America as the place to go to build a future.

Passing into Eternity

In the mid-1800s, immigrants came to the United States from England, Ireland, Scotland, Sweden, Finland, Denmark, Norway,

Opposite: A view from Gibraltar Rock in Columbia County

Americans of German descent take great pride in celebrating their traditions.

and the many different regions that made up Germany. They were drawn to the Midwest by stories of fertile land and the prospect of religious freedom.

Wisconsin attracted more German immigrants than any other national group. They began to arrive in about 1845, in response to pamphlets praising Wisconsin. In the 1850s, 10 percent of all the German immigrants who came to the United States headed for Wisconsin. By 1890, more than 60 percent of the immigrant population of southeastern Wisconsin was German. In 1900, at least 34 percent of the state's population was originally German. One settler in Wisconsin later wrote that people leaving Germany were regarded as passing "into eternity" because their families and friends would probably never see them again.

In 1829, Charles Borup, a Dane, opened a trading post in the Apostle Islands. Another Dane, living in Watertown, wrote a book extolling the upper Midwest. It was published in Denmark in 1847 and the Danes responded. Toward the end of the century, Racine County had more Danes living in it than any comparable part of the country. They introduced kringle, a popular flat, fruit-filled sweet pastry.

Meatpacker Patrick Cudahy built an entire community south of Milwaukee to house the thousands of workers he recruited from Poland in 1893. Cudahy himself was an immigrant from Ireland.

Some groups of newcomers tried to isolate themselves from everyone else. The Norwegians, for example, quickly built their own churches and schools. Otto Tank tried to establish a Moravian community in Ephraim in Door County. The Moravian Church was a Norwegian church that sent missionaries around the world to establish its religious communities.

Immigrants from Wales tended to stay by themselves, building churches in which only Welsh was spoken. They resented the Eng-

Polish Americans in Milwaukee enjoy Polish Fest each June.

lish settlers and tried to maintain their own closed communities. Swedes, on the other hand, were eager to mix and learn English.

The Freed African-Americans

Between the time Wisconsin became a state and the end of the Civil War, about 100 former slaves established a colony in Grant County. Most of these people had been brought to Wisconsin by their owners, who freed them. These African-Americans sought others in the same situation and established the village of Pleasant Ridge. Its school had a black teacher, and several black members were on the school board. Many of the men in the village enlisted to fight in the Civil War.

Freed slaves traveled north to Wisconsin to begin a new life.

Soon after Wisconsin became a state, a bill intended to give African-Americans the right to vote was introduced in Wisconsin's fledgling legislature. To become law, however, the bill had to be approved by a majority of those who voted on the issue. On Election Day in 1849, many people just left that voting space blank. Even though there were numerous votes in favor of the bill, the number of blank votes caused the bill to be defeated.

But that didn't end the matter. In 1865, Ezekiel Gillispie of Milwaukee tried to register to vote. He was refused because he was black. His attorney took the issue to the state supreme court. The judges decided that African-Americans had been given the right to vote in 1849, but the vote had been wrongly counted.

Wisconsinites also defied the Fugitive Slave Act, which required that runaway slaves be returned to their owners in the South. When escaped slave Joshua Glover's owner found him in Racine, a band of angry men broke Glover out of prison and whisked him off to safety in Canada. The state supreme court eventually declared that the Fugitive Slave Act was unconstitutional.

The Civil War

When the Civil War began in 1861, Wisconsin had been a state for only a few years. Many of its immigrant residents were not interested, and some even opposed the state's support of the Union. Some older militia units suddenly found reasons to disband so that they would not be taken into the Union army.

Such opposition did not last long. As the weeks passed, enthusiasm for joining the Union army spread. Many U.S.-born and German men joined the effort. Virtually the entire population of

General William Tecumseh Sherman

African-American men living in Wisconsin served in the Civil War.

Three regiments from Wisconsin, plus one from Indiana, were organized early in the war—the only brigade made up completely of men from what was regarded as the West. They were called the Black Hat Brigade but soon acquired the name Iron Brigade. They were widely known for their bravery—and the huge losses they suffered—during the three days of the bloody Battle of Gettysburg.

Other Wisconsin regiments fought in the Battle of Shiloh in Tennessee and saw action only along the Mississippi River. Wisconsin infantry and cavalry marched through Georgia with General William Tecumseh Sherman and captured Atlanta.

Starting a Political Party

Alvan Bovay of Ripon, encouraged by New York newspaperman Horace Greeley, called a meeting on February 28, 1854, of all those who opposed the Kansas-Nebraska Bill. This bill, making its way through Congress in Washington, D.C., gave each new state the right to decide for itself whether or not it would allow slavery.

Bovay and Greeley knew that some territories west of the Mississippi River were just waiting to join the United States as slave states. Greeley and his peers, however, were opposed to allowing any new slave states into the Union.

Many residents of Ripon attended Bovay's meeting at the village schoolhouse. They voted to form a new political party to oppose slavery. The following July, a larger meeting with a similar purpose was held in Jackson, Michigan. Those attending voted to call themselves "Republicans." To Wisconsinites, however, the meeting in Ripon—which came first—was the founding of the Republican Party. ▪

Old Abe, the Civil War Eagle

The mascot of the Eighth Regiment of the Wisconsin Volunteer Infantry was a bald eagle named Old Abe (right). For four years, the Eighth Wisconsin campaigned through the states around the Mississippi River. The bird himself was smart enough to take cover when the guns roared, but when they stopped, he climbed back onto the perch carried by the official eagle-bearer.

After the war, Old Abe was kept in a two-room suite in the basement of the capitol for seventeen years. He was often taken outside in nice weather, especially for fund-raising fairs and Fourth of July events.

Reporters came to see Old Abe and made up so many tales of the bird's exploits that no one knew what to believe. He was particularly popular at the Centennial celebrations in Philadelphia in 1876.

As Abe aged, he began to get cranky. On March 26, 1881, after inhaling smoke from a small fire in the capitol, he died. The famous bird's body was stuffed and displayed in Madison for many years until a fire destroyed the display. The bird's image lived on as the symbol of the 101st Airborne Division in World War II. The men in the division called themselves "The Screaming Eagles." ▪

It has been estimated that 1 out of every 9 of the 775,000 residents of the state served in the Union army. And at least 1 out of every 9 of those who served died as a result.

Immigration Begins Again

A second wave of immigration began after the Civil War. Railroad building also began again, opening up northwestern Wisconsin. People rushed in to buy the land. Towns sprouted up along the railroad lines.

Not all Americans—or even all Wisconsinites—welcomed this massive immigration. In 1889, the state legislature was controlled

Because large numbers of immigrants came to Wisconsin, many of the state's schools are bilingual today.

by people who wanted "America for the Americans." They passed a law that required classes in all public schools to be taught in English. Immigrants, particularly Germans, were furious. They voted out the state officials who had been in office since the Civil War and voted in George Peck, a humor writer and Milwaukee mayor, to serve as governor.

During that same period, industry grew rapidly, along with the number of industrial workers. Many of them, especially the skilled German and Scandinavian laborers, tried to form unions that would empower the workers against the managers. In 1886, riots broke out among groups of laboring men who were fighting for an eight-hour workday. (Workers that time regularly worked twelve or more hours a day.) Militia companies were soon called out to guard the factories, and one group of soldiers fired into the crowd, killing four men and a young boy.

The entire nation began to oppose poor labor conditions and corruption in government and business. Some people, called Socialists, thought that the government should control business. Victor Berger of Milwaukee became the first Socialist to be elected to the U.S. Congress. During that same period, the city elected two Socialist mayors, including Daniel Hoan, who served for twenty-four years.

The New Century

When World War I started in 1914, Germany was considered an enemy of the United States. The German people of Wisconsin were shocked when they were suddenly regarded as traitors. Some people of German ancestry changed their names to prove that they were loyal Americans.

One of the main obstacles to Wisconsin's participation in the war was Robert M. La Follette, the state's Republican senator in Washington, D.C. He refused to vote in favor of preparing for war. Every time the issue arose, he voted for strict neutrality.

Some Wisconsinites were afraid that other Americans would regard them as favoring Germany, so they decided to root out pro-German feelings. In small towns, some people were charged in court with saying things that favored Germany. Under the Espionage Act, some were fined, and a few even went to federal prison.

The Bad Times

Soon after World War I ended in 1918, the Eighteenth Amendment, called Prohibition, made it illegal to sell alcoholic beverages in the United States. The Germans in America were widely known for

The Prime Minister

Golda Mabovich (back row, second from left) was born in Ukraine in 1898. Anti-Semitism—or hatred of Jews—drove her family to emigrate to the United States. They came to Milwaukee. Although her parents at first opposed the idea, Goldie (a nickname) studied to become a teacher. She taught briefly in Milwaukee. Goldie soon became a Zionist, believing that Jews should have a homeland. After marrying Morris Meyerson, another Zionist, Goldie and Morris moved to Palestine, the British-controlled area that would become Israel.

During the 1920s and 1930s, Golda Meyerson (a name she eventually changed to the more Hebrew "Meir") worked toward the founding of a Jewish nation. She became so important among the Zionists that when Israel was founded as a nation in 1948, she signed the Israeli Declaration of Independence.

For the next twenty-five years, Golda Meir served in the Knesset, the Israeli legislature. In 1969, she was elected to be Israel's fourth prime minister. Meir served for five years before resigning. ■

making beer, and some people think that if Germany had not been the enemy in World War I, Prohibition would never have been approved. The new law put an end to German control of Milwaukee. Thousands of people who worked in the breweries or saloons were now unemployed. Some people felt that, through Prohibition, the government might begin to limit their personal freedoms. Others resented the law for putting them out of work. In 1933, the American people voted to repeal Prohibition.

When the Great Depression began in 1929, more than half of Wisconsin's people found themselves unemployed. In 1932, the state passed the nation's first unemployment insurance law. It required that companies put money into a fund that would continue to provide an employee's salary if that person were laid off from work. It was another three years before the nation as a whole had unemployment insurance.

Wisconsin had undergone many changes since becoming a state. The most profound changes occurred as Wisconsin led the nation into the modern world.

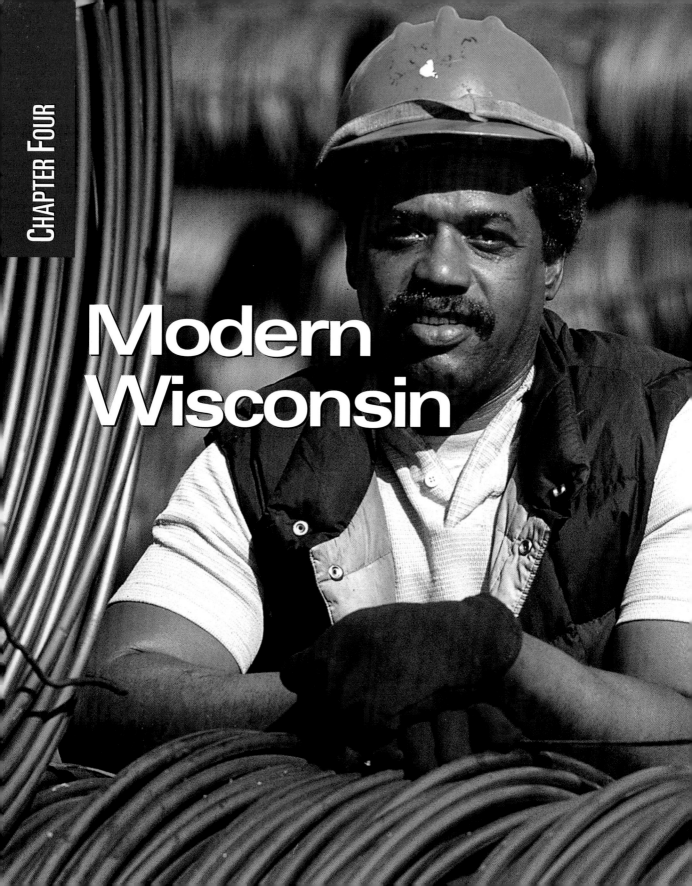

CHAPTER FOUR

Modern Wisconsin

isconsin and the rest of America recovered quickly from the Depression when World War II (1939–1945) began. Suddenly there was work for everyone.

Once again, however, Germany was the enemy. When it became clear that the United States would enter the war, the German-American people of Milwaukee acted early to avoid being regarded as traitors by holding anti-Nazi rallies.

Few people in Wisconsin opposed the war after the Japanese bombed Pearl Harbor in 1941. The United States then declared war on Japan. Both Japan and Germany became the enemies. More than 300,000 men and women from Wisconsin served in the armed forces during World War II.

Wisconsin was already a major producer of industrial machinery, so it was not difficult for the state to adapt its industry to production for war. Some of its products were fairly unusual, however. Many miles from the ocean, for example, three of Wisconsin's cities built ships during the war. Manitowoc, on Lake Michigan's shore, produced submarines for the U.S. Navy. The submarines were towed through Illinois waterways to the Mississippi River. The cities of Superior on Lake Superior and Sturgeon Bay on Green Bay also produced small naval vessels.

World War II memorabilia is on display at the Maritime Museum in Manitowoc.

Opposite: Worker for the Port of Milwaukee

Joseph R. McCarthy

A Sad Episode in American History

Starting in 1950, Joseph R. McCarthy, Wisconsin's Republican senator, began the endeavor that linked his name to an unfortunate era of U.S. history. A lawyer from Appleton, McCarthy discovered that he could accuse opponents of wrongdoing and few people would question him.

McCarthy was elected to the U.S. Senate in 1946, defeating Robert M. La Follette Jr. in the Republican primary. After World War II, many American citizens began to fear the Communist Soviet Union's growing power. McCarthy preyed on that fear by accusing people in the U.S. State Department—and in many other places—of belonging to, or sympathizing with, the Communist Party. He had no real facts, but the accusations gained him the attention he wanted.

People began to be afraid of McCarthy because his accusations threatened their jobs. The Korean War (1950–1953), which pitted the United Nations against Communist North Korea, increased people's fear. In 1954, McCarthy attacked the U.S. Army's leadership. The U.S. Senate held televised hearings to question the people McCarthy had accused. For the first time, millions of Americans watched McCarthy bully the people he was accusing instead of letting them answer his questions.

McCarthy's support gradually dwindled. The U.S. Senate voted to censure, or reprimand, McCarthy for his behavior. In April 1957,

Wisconsin's infamous senator died. The word "McCarthyism" now refers to the use of unfair tactics and reckless accusations.

Hispanics in Wisconsin

Few Hispanics lived in Wisconsin in the early years of the state. In the 1920s, however, industry and agriculture were doing so well that Hispanics were actively recruited for jobs in manufacturing and harvesting.

A Folklorico dancer at the annual Mexican Fiesta in Milwaukee

Mexicans began arriving in Wisconsin to work the sugar-beet fields after Congress passed a tax on sugar imported from other countries. This type of agriculture lasted in the state only as long as the law did, but there were other crops for migrant workers to harvest. Thousands of workers came to Wisconsin each year to pick crops. Labor conditions for these migrant workers were horrendous. Hours were long and the pay was very low. Often, whole families picked crops, but only the fathers were paid.

In 1966, Mexican-American migrant workers marched from Wautoma to Madison, calling for respect and recognition. Their leader was 22-year-old Jesús Salás, a student at the university in Madison and the son of a migrant worker who had managed to buy a farm near Wautoma. The march was successful. By the following spring, most migrant workers were earning at least the minimum wage. In the long run, though, they lost the struggle. Machines swiftly began to replace migrant workers.

Since 1976, state law has required that bilingual (two-language) classes be available in school districts with Hispanic populations.

African-Americans in Milwaukee

A chapter of the National Association for the Advancement of Colored People (NAACP) formed in Milwaukee as early as 1919. Few people in Milwaukee paid any attention because they thought racism existed only in the South. They ignored the fact that an increasing number of African-Americans living in Milwaukee had to live in a small, poor section of the city. A ghetto, called the Inner Core, had formed in Milwaukee.

After World War II, many African-American people were earning a good living and were able to afford better housing. But in Milwaukee, no one would sell them property that was outside the ghetto area.

This segregation in the community created segregated schools. Black children and white children went to different schools. In 1954, the U.S. Supreme Court ruled that racial segregation in schools was unconstitutional. Despite this ruling, the Milwaukee School Board did nothing to solve the problem.

In 1956, Vel Phillips, a Milwaukee woman, became the first woman and the first African-American elected to serve on Milwaukee's city council. Phillips was on the council when African-Americans in the city sought open-housing laws. Such laws would

In 1967, schoolchildren protested school segregation in Milwaukee.

Father James Groppi holding a prayer vigil in Milwaukee

have required landlords to rent or sell to anyone, not just to white people. But Phillips was unable to persuade the council to act.

Racial tension continued to mount. In July 1967, an eight-day riot of violence and destruction erupted in the Inner Core. Many houses were burned and three people were killed.

Father James Groppi, a white Catholic priest, led protest marches throughout the city, trying to force the Milwaukee government to pass open-housing laws. They marched again and again for 200 days. In response some changes were made, but the city council refused to vote for open housing.

In 1968, Dr. Martin Luther King Jr., the famed African-American civil rights leader, was assassinated in Memphis, Tennessee. Immediately, the federal government passed strong open-housing laws. After Father Groppi and student protestors took over the capitol in Madison, Milwaukee also passed open-housing laws. Even so, Wisconsin's largest city remained one of the most racially segregated in the nation. Milwaukee schools remained segregated until a court ordered them to be desegregated in 1979.

DRUMS for the Menominee

The Menominees protesting in Madison in 1971

In the early 1950s, the U.S. government decided to "terminate" some of the reservations established for Native Americans. This decision broke agreements that had been made in treaties a century earlier.

The Menominee people voted to accept termination of the reservation and of the rights accorded to them as a federally recognized tribe. They established Menominee Enterprises Incorporated (MEI) as owner of the forest and the sawmills on this land. Each Menominee received 100 shares in MEI plus a negotiable bond valued at $3,000, issued in the name of MEI. Outsiders also owned shares in MEI. Tribal members voted to turn their valuable land into Wisconsin's seventy-second county.

The plan sounded good, but Menominee County quickly became the poorest county in the state. The Menominee lost all federal fishing rights, medical care, and educational grants. Individuals who had no income found they had to start paying property taxes. The outsiders who controlled MEI developed part of the county as a resort—without getting the approval of the Menominee shareholders.

An organization called DRUMS (Determination of Rights and Unity for Menominee Shareholders) started protesting. In 1971, DRUMS activists marched 222 miles (357 km) to Madison to urge the state to reestablish the land as a Menominee reservation.

The termination of reservation rights wasn't working well anywhere. The federal government announced that the policy itself would be terminated. Wisconsin's two senators, Gaylord Nelson and William Proxmire, introduced a bill in Congress that would return the Menominee to federally recognized tribal status. In 1975, the government reestablished the Menominee reservation.

Today, the Menominee are known nationwide for managing their forests in a way that brings praise from environmentalists. They also earn considerable money from the gaming casino they opened at Keshena—the first one in Wisconsin.

**A Potawatomi
casino**

Casinos and Gambling

The Wisconsin constitution originally outlawed gambling. During Prohibition, when the sale of alcoholic beverages was outlawed, many tucked-away resorts in Wisconsin sold alcoholic drinks and offered gambling on the sly, too. That kind of resort disappeared after alcohol became legal again in 1933. Since 1965, bit by bit, the state constitution has been amended to allow a variety of games of chance. In 1987, a state lottery was approved.

In 1988, the U.S. Congress passed the Indian Gaming Regulatory Act. This law allowed gambling in casinos on Native American land, but required that the profits benefit the tribe as a whole. Other tribes, seeing how much income the Menominee earn from their casino, have also opened casinos and bingo parlors. Many tribes are using this income to build roads, schools, and medical centers on the reservations.

Wisconsin Works

Some people are unable to earn enough money to support themselves and their families. People can have trouble earning a living for many different reasons. Single women who have small children, for example, sometimes cannot afford to pay someone to watch their children while they work. Some workers are trained to do specific jobs. If these jobs are filled or become obsolete, these workers may have difficulty finding new jobs. Other people are ill or

Earth Day

In the 1960s, Senator Gaylord Nelson of Wisconsin watched as students nationwide protested the Vietnam War. He realized that their practice of holding special days called teach-ins might work for another cause—protection of the environment. The first Earth Day took place on April 21, 1970. An estimated 20 million Americans participated in demonstrations, classes, and activities (above) focused on preserving the planet's environment. Earth Day has been held annually since then. Gaylord Nelson later wrote: "It was truly an astonishing grassroots explosion. The people cared, and Earth Day became the first opportunity they ever had to join in a nationwide demonstration to send a big message to the politicians—a message to tell them to wake up and do something." ▪

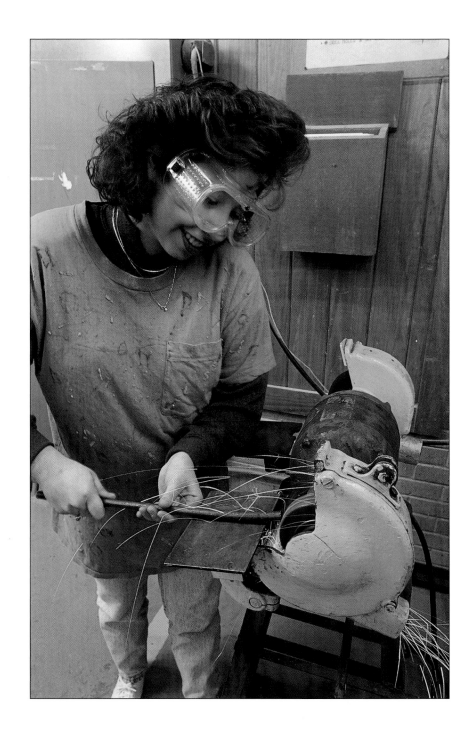

To get people off welfare, Wisconsin initiated a program aimed at teaching people new skills and placing them in jobs.

have disabilities. Most states use tax dollars to support welfare programs that help such people by paying their basic living expenses, but taxpayers often object to supporting people who receive welfare year after year.

In 1993, Wisconsin introduced several programs designed to reduce the cost of welfare. Then, in 1996, the state legislature introduced a program called Wisconsin Works. This program does everything possible to help people find new ways to support themselves and their families. Wisconsin Works includes plans for teaching people new skills. The program pays child-care costs so that parents of young children can go to work. It also helps people with transportation costs and it gives companies payments, called subsidies, to help with the cost of training new workers.

Impressed by the Wisconsin initiative, the U.S. Congress instituted a similar nationwide program in 1997. Both the Wisconsin and the national programs will have to be in effect for several years before we know if they really do help people earn an adequate income. Once again, Wisconsin is in the lead in developing programs that affect the people of the state and nation.

The Land: A Product of Ice

Hiking through Kettle Moraine State Forest

Opposite: The Mississippi River Valley from Eagle Bluff

Four times in the last million years, Earth's climate has gradually turned colder. Huge sheets of ice, or glaciers, expanded southward from the Arctic Circle. Each one covered much of Wisconsin. The landscape we see today is the result of the last glacier, which began to form about 70,000 years ago. Called the Wisconsin glacier, the 400-foot (122-m)-thick layer of ice retreated about 10,000 years ago.

As the glacier grew and spread southward, it crushed and moved everything in its path. Well, not quite everything—the southward flow of the glacier was controlled by hard rock that it could not crush. The 70-mile (112-km)-long Door Peninsula sticking out into Lake Michigan is a wedge of such hard rock called the Niagara Escarpment.

When the planet began to warm again, the leading, or southern, edge of the glacier began to retreat. It left a pile of debris called the glacier's *terminal moraine.* As the ice cap gradually melted, trickles of water seeped through the glacier, creating holes. Rocks fell through the holes, forming cone-shaped mounds that were left behind as the glacier retreated. These mounds, called *kames,* are features of Kettle Moraine State Forest. One of the highest, near Hartford, is called Holy Hill because of the large Roman Catholic monastery and shrine that stand on top of it.

Long mounds called *drumlins* and round ponds called *kettles* are also found in the Kettle Moraine area. The *eskers* are ridges of sand and gravel formed by the rivers running under the melting glacier that carried sediment with them.

Where the Glacier Missed

Only a small portion of the state, in the south and central west, was never covered by the glaciers. Called the Driftless Area, it is higher than the rest of the state. Instead of covering these hills, the glacial ice split and rejoined in northern Illinois. Unlike most of Wisconsin, the Driftless Area has no lakes but it has wide, flat-bottomed valleys, called *coulees*.

The ancient Baraboo Hills created a natural dam, so as the glacier melted, water was trapped by the hills and formed a huge lake. Geologists call it Glacial Lake Wisconsin. Spectacular Devil's Lake formed in the "hole" in the Baraboo Hills that remained after the lake flowed away.

Glacial Lake Wisconsin drained away in one huge catastrophic flow that formed the channel through which the Wisconsin River now flows. The extraordinarily beautiful Wisconsin Dells were created when the flowing water undermined sand-

Signs of the Ice

In 1971, Wisconsin, working with the federal government and various local governments, created the first Ice Age National Scientific Reserve. The reserve, which is part of the National Park System, spans the state in nine state parks that preserve features left by the glacier. The 1,000-mile (1,600-km) trail (above) winds through a dramatic landscape built by the glacier. The trail runs from Potawatomi State Park at Sturgeon Bay to Interstate Park on the border with Minnesota. ■

stone, creating huge bluffs that line the river. In its wake, the ca-
tastrophe also left a huge, flat sand-covered area that has been
called the sand counties.

**Devil's Door at Devil's
Lake near Baraboo**

Today's Land

There are no mountains, deserts, or other extremes in modern
Wisconsin. Instead, Wisconsin has a little bit of everything that
makes a land livable.

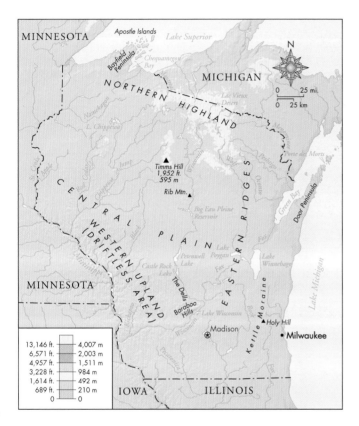

MINNESOTA Apostle Islands Lake Superior

MICHIGAN

NORTHERN HIGHLAND

Timms Hill
1,952 ft.
595 m

Rib Mtn.

Big Eau Pleine
Reservoir

CENTRAL PLAIN

WESTERN UPLAND (DRIFTLESS AREA)

EASTERN RIDGES

Lake
Petenwell
Castle Rock
Lake

The Dells

Baraboo
Hills

Lake Wisconsin

Lake
Poygan

Lake
Winnebago

Green Bay

Door Peninsula

Lake Michigan

Kettle Moraine

Holy Hill

Madison

Milwaukee

MINNESOTA

13,146 ft. — 4,007 m
6,571 ft. — 2,003 m
4,957 ft. — 1,511 m
3,228 ft. — 984 m
1,614 ft. — 492 m
689 ft. — 210 m
0 — 0

IOWA   ILLINOIS

N

0   25 mi.
0   25 km

**Wisconsin's
topography**

The highest part of the state is in the north-central region. From there, the land slopes downward to the south, east, and west.

A low plain lies along Lake Superior, but about 10 or 20 miles (16 to 32 km) inland a ridge, or escarpment, rises 300 to 400 feet (91 to 122 m). Beautiful waterfalls form there as the Black, Brule, and other rivers flow over it. The escarpment defines the edge of a large, high region called the Northern Highland, which has an average elevation of 1,700 feet (518 m) above sea level. The Northern Highland is a region of poor soils and vast wetlands, unsuitable for much agriculture but great for the forests called the North Woods.

South of the Northern Highland is the Central Plain. Tough sandstone shapes that have resisted the effects of time and weather jut out from this plain. West of the Central Plain lies the Western Upland, rugged land that was not smoothed by glacial action. Its splendid valleys and high hills are usually dotted with cattle.

East and south of the Central Plain are the Eastern Ridges and Lowlands. They extend from Door County to the Illinois border and across to the Mississippi River. Much of this region features landforms left by the retreating glaciers.

The Great Lakes

About 673 miles (1,083 km) of Wisconsin borders on Lake Michigan and Lake Superior, the Great Lakes that were carved out by the Wisconsin glacier. Most of Lake Michigan's western shore belongs to Wisconsin. The major feature on the Lake Michigan shoreline is Door Peninsula, which forms Green Bay.

The High Spots

The highest—and the second highest—peaks in Wisconsin are both in Price County. Timms Hill is 1,951 feet (595 m), and Pearson Hill is only 1 foot (30 cm) lower. Sugarbush Hill in Forest County drops down to 1,939 feet (591 m). Rib Mountain, in Marathon County near Wausau, is a single mountain of rock that jutted up in Precambrian times. Rib Mountain is the fourth-highest mountain in the state at 1,924 feet (586 m). ■

Aldo Leopold

Recognized as one of the founders of the environmental movement in the United States, Aldo Leopold was born in Iowa in 1886. Leopold was a forester with the U.S. Forest Service. His survey of game animals so impressed the University of Wisconsin that he was invited to become Professor of Game Management. He turned the program into a wildlife management program.

Leopold's fame as an environmentalist stems from *A Sand County Almanac,* a book of essays written during the many years he and his family vacationed at "The Shack," an old farm in Sauk County on the Wisconsin River. Only moderately popular when the book was published a few months after Leopold's death in 1948, it has since become basic reading for people who care about the environment. ■

Lake Superior, known to Native Americans as Gitche Gumee, is the largest freshwater lake in the world and is famous for its violent storms. When iron ore was being mined in the Hurley area in the 1880s, hundreds of ore-carrying ships sailed out of the cities of Superior and Duluth. Many of them went to the bottom of the lake in great storms. That isn't all old-time history—the *Edmund Fitzgerald* sank in 1975, prompting Canadian singer Gordon Lightfoot to write a ballad about the event.

Twenty-two islands carved out by winds and waves off Bayfield Peninsula are called the Apostle Islands. They were named by French explorers who saw only twelve islands and named them for Jesus Christ's twelve disciples, or apostles. The smaller islands, which are part of the Apostle Islands National Lakeshore, have no roads, but they are open to hikers. Many of them are edged by dramatic cliffs.

The Wisconsin River

The Wisconsin River is generally divided into the Lower, Middle, and Upper Rivers. On its 430-mile (692-km) journey to the Mississippi, the Wisconsin River drops 917 feet (280 m), sometimes in spectacular waterfalls, sometimes in vast sluggish lakes called *flowages.*

The Upper River, from its headwaters in Lac Vieux Desert (Old Desert Lake) on the Wisconsin-Michigan border, extends through lumbering country to Plover, where it makes a quick jog—first east and then west. The Upper River is notorious for the root-beer color of its water. It flows through forests of tamarack, a

Limestone caves add beauty and mystery to the Apostle Islands National Lakeshore.

conifer in the larch family, that deposit a brown chemical called tannin in its waters.

The Middle River extends from the fast-moving Wisconsin Rapids through the beautiful twisting gorge called the Wisconsin Dells. The river then stretches eastward again to Portage, where it joins the Fox River.

The Lower River, the region that was settled first, extends from Portage southwestward through the Driftless Area to just south of Prairie du Chien. There it flows into the Mississippi River, becoming part of the "father of waters." The bluffs of the Mississippi and Wisconsin Rivers provide soaring sites for many bald eagles.

Lakes and Swamps

Wisconsin has almost 15,000 lakes, including many kettles carved out by the retreating glacier. Some of these lakes have not yet been mapped and measured. Together, Wisconsin's lakes total almost 1 million acres (404,700 ha). They are concentrated in three areas: north of Rhinelander near the headwaters of the Wisconsin River; farther northwest near Hayward; and at the southern part of the state west of Milwaukee. Vilas County alone has at least 1,300 lakes.

The Amnicon Falls on the Amnicon River

Lake Winnebago is the largest lake that lies entirely within Wisconsin's borders. Formed in the Fox Valley, it has been filled by the Fox and Wolf Rivers until it is 28 miles (45 km) long and 10 miles (16 km) wide. Lake Winnebago is very shallow, however—20 feet (6 m) deep at most. Several cities developed on the western shore, but the eastern shore is an escarpment that prevents people from reaching the water.

Originally, the central part of the state was a vast swamp, or wetland. There, the Native Americans picked blueberries and wild

Opposite: In the Wisconsin Dells, the gorge called "Witch's Gulf" takes many twists and turns.

Wisconsin's Geographical Features

Total area; rank	65,500 sq. mi. (105,412 sq km); 22nd
Land; rank	54,314 sq. mi. (87,410 sq km); 25th
Water; rank	11,186 sq. mi. (18,002 sq km); 3rd
Inland water; **rank**	1,831 sq. mi. (2,947 sq km); 11th
Great Lakes; **rank**	9,355 sq. mi. (15,055 sq km); 2nd
Geographic center	Wood, 9 miles (14 km) southeast of Marshfield
Highest point	Timms Hill, 1,952 feet (595 m)
Lowest point	581 feet (177 m) along Lake Michigan
Largest city	Milwaukee
Longest river	Wisconsin River, 430 miles (692 km)
Population; rank	4,906,745 (1990 census); 16th
Record high temperature	114°F (46°C) at Wisconsin Dells on July 13, 1936
Record low temperature	–54°F (–48°C) at Vanderbilt on January 24, 1922
Average July temperature	70°F (21°C)
Average January temperature	14°F (–10°C)
Average annual precipitation	31 inches (79 cm)

rice and hunted muskrat, beaver, and other fur-bearing animals. However, as the settlers arrived in large numbers, several million acres of wetland were drained and filled in for farmland.

Horicon Marsh near Waupun is a 50-square-mile (129-sq-km) basin that filled in with water as the glacier retreated. The Rock River, which runs through the marsh, was briefly dammed, creating a lake, but in 1941, the federal and state governments took over and let it turn back into wetland. Each year, the Horicon National Wildlife Refuge attracts millions of migrating Canada geese.

The Horicon National Wildlife Refuge provides a stopping place for Canada geese during their annual migrations.

Climate

Wisconsin extends from the Illinois border up to the Apostle Islands in Lake Superior. This location gets weather that varies greatly from winter to summer. It can be bitterly cold with lots of snow in winter, and its summers are warm and humid. This type of climate is called temperate continental.

Three different types of air masses affect Wisconsin. The Continental Polar air masses from the Northwest bring bitter-cold, dry weather in winter. The Maritime Tropical Gulf air mass from the Gulf of Mexico brings high humidity and heat in summer. The Maritime Polar Pacific air mass can bring more moderate weather straight from the west at any time during the year.

Wisconsin's weather is also much affected by the Great Lakes on its northern and eastern sides. These lakes moderate the weather in the coastal areas, which are warmer in winter and cooler in summer than the rest of the state. However, residents of shoreline cities also get lake-effect snow. In winter, they may have several inches of snow while 30 miles (48 km) inland, the sky is sunny and nobody needs to shovel.

Cross-country skiing is a popular winter sport of Wisconsinites and tourists alike.

The southern counties get about 30 inches (76 cm) of snow each winter. The annual snowfall in Iron County, to the north, can be as much as 100 inches (254 cm). The most rain to fall in a single day was 11.72 inches (29.77 cm) at Mellen on June 24, 1946.

On average, about nineteen tornadoes touch down in Wisconsin each year. The twisters come from the west, and primarily strike the southwestern corner of the state, especially in late spring and early summer. The worst tornado in recent years struck in Barneveld, west of Madison, in 1984. The violent, spiraling wind touched down on the central business district and ploughed along the main street, destroying everything in its path.

Wildlife

As the Wisconsin glacier retreated, large mammals as well as trees and other plants that inhabited the southern part of the continent quickly found new homes farther north. About 1830, when settlers began to arrive, approximately 63 percent of the state was covered by forests. Most of the remaining land was open prairie. The prairie disappeared as the land was cleared for agriculture.

Trappers had already reduced the population of small fur-bearing mammals, but the settlers found bears, Canada lynx, and wolves. Bears are still found in the North Woods, but the lynx, wolf, and pine marten are now on the state's endangered-species list. There are so many white-tailed deer that they often fall prey to speeding cars on highways. In 1995, a first attempt was made to reintroduce elk to northern Wisconsin.

The Woodland people regularly burned the land to keep it fertile. This kept the southern part of the state treeless. It wasn't until

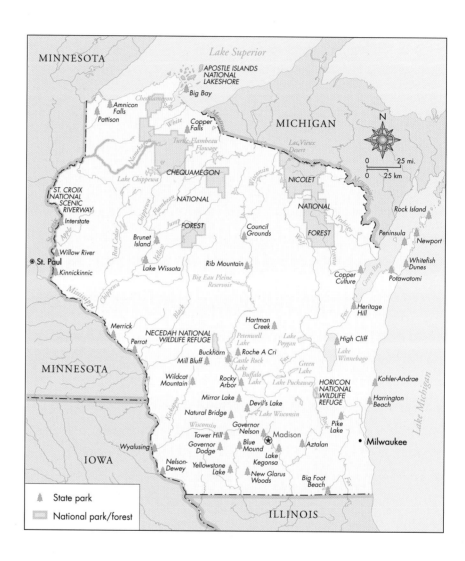

Wisconsin's parks and forests

European settlers arrived that oaks, maples, and other hardwood trees began to grow. Even then, most of them were cut down to create farmland.

Today's North Woods reflect the fact that the old first-growth trees were cleared long ago by loggers working for the big timber barons. Many pines have been replanted, and aspen and birch have grown tall in the area called Cutover. Their golden leaves makes the whole region glow in the autumn sunshine.

Wisconsin has protected a considerable amount of its own land for its people. It has forty-seven state parks, nine state forests, fourteen state trails, and four recreation areas. The largest state park is Devil's Lake, which encompasses about 10,000 acres (4,047 ha). The smallest is Heritage Hill, with only 50 acres (20 ha). There are also two national forests (which are not necessarily full of trees) in Wisconsin—Nicolet and Chequamegon.

Windsurfing at Egg Harbor in Door County

John Muir of the Redwoods

Eleven-year-old John Muir emigrated with his family from Scotland to a farm in Marquette County in 1849. He gloried in the wilderness he explored there on Fountain Lake. After attending the University of Wisconsin, he set off across America, walking everywhere he went. Settling in Yosemite Valley, California, Muir helped influence Congress to pass the Yosemite National Park Bill of 1890, which created both Yosemite and Sequoia National Parks. He also helped persuade President Theodore Roosevelt to set aside 148 million acres (60 million ha) for forest reserves and national parks. Two years later, Muir founded the Sierra Club, one of the most influential organizations of the environmental protection movement in the United States. In 1908, the United States named Muir Woods National Monument in western California in honor of this dedicated environmentalist. ■

CHAPTER SIX

Around Wisconsin

U sing the southeast corner as our starting point, let's make a counterclockwise tour of the state. Bear in mind that Native Americans, French explorers, and European settlers named most places in Wisconsin.

The cities of Kenosha, Racine, and Milwaukee can be regarded as parts of the giant metropolitan area of Chicago, which extends up the shore of Lake Michigan. Kenosha is a thriving city with its front door on Lake Michigan, where people come to fish. Its back door is a major shopping area visited by people from all over the Midwest. Nearby, at Bristol, a major Renaissance Fair is held in a beautiful wooded area every weekend during the summer.

Racine, a few miles up the shoreline, is the home of S. C. Johnson Wax, makers of numerous products for the home. The J. I. Case Company of Racine, established in 1844, is one of the largest manufacturers of farming implements in the world. In 1933, Western Publishing Company of Racine brought Walt Disney to the public in the form of coloring books and the popular "Little Big Books." Ten years later, they started publishing the Little Golden Books, which have sold more than a billion copies.

The former Coast Guard station at Racine

Opposite: The Milwaukee skyline at the Milwaukee River

Milwaukee, the German City

Milwaukee was founded in 1795 as a trading post run by Jacques Vieau at the junction of the Kinnickinnic, Menominee, and Milwaukee Rivers. Settlers from New England arrived in 1833 when it was part of Michigan Territory.

Almost from the start, it was clear that Milwaukee would be big. To begin with, the city's economy did not depend on just one industry. It was a port city as well as a major producer of clothing, iron, furniture, flour, shoes, and construction materials. One of those building materials was the yellow-colored brick that gave Milwaukee the nickname "Cream City."

The first brewery in Milwaukee was actually owned by a Welshman but, in 1848, Germans began to immigrate in large numbers.

Three Men and Milwaukee

In 1833, the first white settlers arrived at the river junction that would become Milwaukee. They used gravel hills that had been left behind by the glaciers to fill in much of the swampland and then built on it. Byron Kilbourn from Connecticut arrived the following spring and set up a real-estate business. However, the best land—east of the river—had already been claimed by Solomon Juneau in what he called Juneautown. Colonel George Walker also arrived in 1834. He settled on the point at the mouth of the Menominee River, which became Walker's Point and the South Side. Kilbourn, Juneau, and Walker thus became competing founders of Milwaukee.

Kilbourn had the advantage because many newcomers arrived by ship, and he sent a steamer out to bring the people to the West Side. He also built a road from the bridge that carried overland travelers from Chicago.

Quite deliberately, Kilbourn prevented his streets, which ended at the Milwaukee River, from lining up with those of Juneautown. Even today, the bridges across the river must be set at an angle to make the streets join. In 1846, the residents voted to join the various parts into one city, which they called Milwaukee, a Potawatomi word meaning "gathering place." Today, more than a million people are gathered in the Milwaukee area. ■

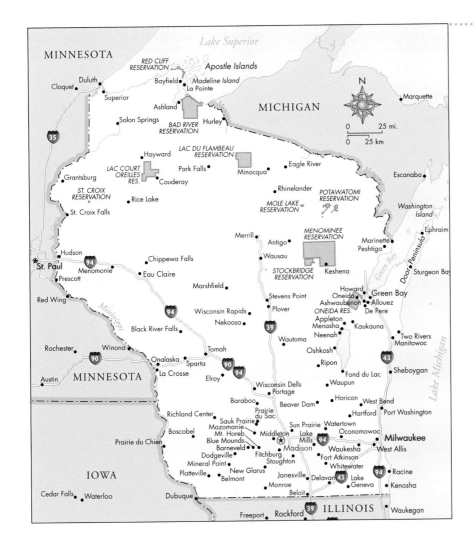

Wisconsin's cities and interstates

Most German immigrants arrived with some money and some business skills. They also knew about the brewing industry. As the twentieth century started, Milwaukee was regarded by many as a foreign city because it was more German than American. Today, in Milwaukee, 30.5 percent of the people are African-American and 10 percent are Polish, but a full 40 percent of the residents are of German heritage.

Among the places that both residents and visitors enjoy are the Milwaukee Public Museum, the Milwaukee County Zoo, and the famed triple geodesic domes of Mitchell Park. One dome contains tropical plants, the second a desert world, and the third varies with the season.

West of Milwaukee

Many lakes of various sizes attract commuters and visitors to the areas southwest, west, and northwest of Milwaukee. The largest of these lakes is Lake Geneva, where many wealthy Chicagoans once built huge homes. The old homes that remain give boaters an idea of the luxurious living of past eras. Many beautiful houses have recently been built there, too. Green Lake, farther north, has a similar history.

Williams Bay on Lake Geneva is the home of Yerkes Observatory, owned by the

University of Chicago. It has the world's largest refracting tele-scope. Edwin Hubble, for whom the Hubble Space Telescope is named, once worked there.

Nearby Delavan, once the center of the circus world, also became the home of Wisconsin's School for the Deaf. It was founded in 1850, when Ebenezer Chesebro turned his own home into a school to help his deaf daughter. When Chesebro could no longer afford to run the school, the state legislature approved funds to support it.

Oconomowoc (probably the only city name that has an "o" as every other letter) has several lakes and a river within it, including Lac La Belle, which means "the beautiful lake."

Along Lake Winnebago

The city at the southern end of Lake Winnebago is called Fond du Lac, meaning "bottom end of the lake." It may have a French

Opposite: The Mitchell Park Conservatory

Population of Wisconsin's Major Cities (1990)

Milwaukee	628,088
Madison	191,262
Green Bay	96,466
Racine	84,298
Kenosha	80,352
Appleton	65,695

The Experimental Aircraft Association Museum in Oshkosh

name, but when the great immigration era ended, more than half the population of Fond du Lac was German.

Oshkosh, the city halfway up the lake, is known worldwide because of the products that come from that city. Trucks, rugged children's clothing, and luggage are among the products with "Oshkosh" in their name. The name, chosen in 1840, belonged to the Menominee chief known as the "bravest of the brave." He was responsible for ensuring that his people kept the rights to their land in Wisconsin.

But to pilots, "Oshkosh" means something else. Each summer, the Experimental Aircraft Association (EAA) which moved to Oshkosh from Hales Corners near Milwaukee, holds the International Fly-In. For two weeks, the EAA's small Wittman Field becomes the busiest airport in the world. The EAA's Air Adventure Museum houses *Voyager*, the only airplane to fly nonstop around the world.

Appleton is at the north end of the lake where the Fox River enters it. The nation's first electric power plant to be run by water was built in Appleton fewer than four weeks after Thomas Edison, inventor of the lightbulb, turned on the first electric power station in New York City in 1882. Appleton is the center of an area called "Paper Valley," which supports many paper mills and related industries.

It is said that the hamburger was invented for the Outagamie County Fair. Outagamie Museum features exhibits related to Harry Houdini, the great magician and escape artist who grew up in Appleton.

Outagamie Museum in Appleton

Between Green Bay and Lake Winnebago, the Fox River drops more than 170 feet (52 m). Originally, the river fell over a series of rapids. Today, the drop is controlled by dams and locks that create the power used by the local paper mills. There are seventeen locks in a distance of only 40 miles (64 km).

Around the Mitten's Thumb

Despite being one of the most popular tourist destinations, Door Peninsula is a quite rural area. It has often been compared to New England in appearance. Because its climate is moderated by both Lake Michigan and Green Bay, the 13-mile (21-km)-wide peninsula is ideal cherry-growing land.

Between the tip of the peninsula and Washington Island lies a treacherous stretch of water where so many boats sank that the French called it *Porte des Morts,* meaning "Death's Door." Fortunately, it was "Door," not "Death," that became part of the name of the peninsula and the county occupying it. Washington

Island has the largest community of people originally from Iceland in the United States.

At the southern end of Green Bay stands the city of Green Bay, the third-largest city in the state. The first settlements in Wisconsin occurred mainly around the end of Green Bay. Heritage Hill State Park at De Pere shows us how those settlers lived. Green Bay itself is well known as "Titletown" for its winning Packers football team. The team is so popular that close to 30,000 people are on the waiting list for season tickets.

North Country

The North Woods begin at Green Bay and cover much of the northern part of the state—wherever there are no lakes or roads. Farming has never been too successful in the north because of the acid soil and the overwhelming number of stumps and rocks. The cities of Rhinelander, Wausau, and Minocqua are at the heart of this logging-turned-recreational area.

Rhinelander is home to the University of Wisconsin Outreach School of the Arts, held every July. It was started by Wisconsin writer Robert Gard. The school attracts hundreds of people from all over the country to its writing and art courses. The Rhinelander Logging Museum is home to both the hodag and a replica of a full logging camp.

The rivers that form the Wisconsin border are prime places for summer cottages. The Montreal River at the western end of the border marked Wisconsin's iron-mining area. The small town of Hurley was once notorious as a place where the miners and loggers could find all the "sin" they wanted in their off-hours. The infamous Chicago gangster Al Capone had a hideaway at Couderay, near Hayward.

Among the fish that people catch in the northern lakes are large muskies (officially known as muskellunge), but none of them is as big as the "fish" that houses the National Freshwater Fishing Hall of Fame in Hayward. The museum is housed inside a giant replica of a muskie that is 143 feet (42 m) long.

The Apostle Islands lie off Bayfield Peninsula. The largest, Madeline Island, is about 13 miles (21 km) long. Its town of La Pointe is the only village on the islands. The island can be

At the Rhinelander Logging Museum, visitors can see trees that are native to Wisconsin.

The National Freshwater Fishing Hall of Fame in Hayward

The Madeline Island ferry

reached by ferry from Bayfield in summer. In winter, the bay freezes over, and it is safe to drive a car across. The "road" across is often marked by old Christmas trees.

Superior is a "twin" city to Duluth, which is on the other side of the border. They share a harbor on St. Louis Bay, which is almost completely enclosed by the protective sandbar called Minnesota Point. Ships can load at Superior for carrying grain or ore through the Great Lakes, down the St. Lawrence Seaway, and then to anywhere in the world. Superior became a shipbuilding city by introducing the whaleback, an unusually shaped—but very efficient—cargo ship. The last whaleback, finished in 1896, was the SS *Meteor,* now a floating museum in Superior.

The beautiful St. Croix River forms part of the boundary between Wisconsin and Minnesota. Numerous parks line this National Scenic River. Interstate Park, formed jointly by the two states, lies on both sides of the river. Big Manitou Falls in Pattison State Park is the state's highest waterfall.

Coulee Country

From Prescott southward, the western border of Wisconsin is the mighty Mississippi River. The Driftless Area that parallels the river contains some of the most spectacular scenery in the state.

While the North Woods are serene and crisp, the hills and bluffs of Coulee Country are majestic.

Lake Pepin is created by the differing flows of the Mississippi and the Chippewa Rivers. The faster-moving Chippewa carries vast amounts of silt and gravel to the Mississippi, where it is deposited, raising the river and spreading it out to form Lake Pepin, which is about 25 miles (40 km) long.

La Crosse, the largest city in western Wisconsin, was named for the Native American game of lacrosse. La Crosse is an important river port and a university city.

Early morning fog spreads over the valleys of Coulee Country near Arcadia.

Many tourists take advantage of Wisconsin's fine golf courses.

Most of the railway tracks in Wisconsin were abandoned in the 1960s and 1970s. About 32 miles (52 km) of track bed, which run through and tunnel between the towns of Elroy and Sparta, were developed into a biking trail. Enjoyed by more than 60,000 people a year, it connects with other trails, making Coulee Country a biker's delight.

The entire region is part of the Upper Mississippi National Wildlife and Fish Refuge. The river is controlled by the U.S. Army Corps of Engineers, which can—and does—affect the river and its wildlife by building dams and locks. The refuge can be explored by driving along the Great River Road.

Along the River—South

History and most people's view of the Wisconsin River begin where the Fox River almost bumps the eastward bend in the Wisconsin, at Portage. Before the river reaches Portage, it goes through the Wisconsin Dells, one of the earliest and largest tourist attractions in the state. The name "Dells" comes from the French word *dalles,* which means "slabs" or "tiles." The Dells are a series of rocky cliffs along the river.

The Winnebago, or Ho-Chunk, called the Dells "the place where the waters clash" and regarded it as holy. Ho-Chunk tradition says that the Great Spirit formed the twisting dells of the

The "Sage of Sauk City"

August Derleth was a prolific writer who recorded the small events of life along the Wisconsin River. He wrote more than 100 books, including *Wind over Wisconsin* (1938) and *Evening in Spring* (1941). In many of his books, Derleth told of life in "Sac Prairie," which was a combination of the twin river towns he lived in—Sauk City and Prairie du Sac. He wrote mostly of his own life on the river, both as a boy and as an observant adult. Derleth also served as editor of Madison's *Capital Times* for twenty years. ■

Wisconsin River by turning into a snake and writhing through the land. Today, water-fun parks, miniature and regular golf courses, and casinos are scattered throughout this beautiful area.

Baraboo is home to the Circus World Museum and the International Crane Foundation (ICF), which is dedicated to preventing the loss of these graceful, long-legged birds. All fifteen known species of cranes are in trouble, and all are represented by the ICF.

Closer to Madison, Norwegian immigrants left their mark in several towns. Early Norwegian life can be seen at Little Norway, near Blue Mounds, west of Madison. Authentic furnishings and beautiful Norwegian art called rosemaling are on display throughout the buildings. Stoughton, south of Madison, hosts *Syttende Mai,* an important Norwegian independence celebration, each year.

Not far away, it was the Swiss instead of the Norwegians who settled the area. The

Little Norway near Blue Mounds

Little Switzerland at New Glarus

hilly town of New Glarus shows the influence of its Swiss founders. The town offers visitors a look at an early Swiss settlement as well as the William Tell Festival, which is held each autumn.

The Kickapoo River Valley, running north from Boscobel on the river, has trim farms, quiet hills, and lovely valleys that make it prime apple-growing country. The fruit from these orchards is sold throughout the country. The Kickapoo tribe moved west before settlers came, but the name lives on.

Looking inside a Stomach

Dr. William Beaumont, an Army surgeon, was stationed on Mackinac Island in 1822 when a French-Canadian voyageur named Alexis St. Martin was brought to him with a gunshot wound in the abdomen. The shot had removed part of St. Martin's abdominal wall, and the wound took nearly a year to heal.

During this time, a small passage remained in the abdominal wall, held closed by surrounding tissue. By pressing on this passage, Beaumont could see the workings of the man's stomach.

St. Martin accompanied Beaumont when the doctor was transferred to Fort Crawford at Prairie du Chien. There, Beaumont experimented by putting various foods into St. Martin's stomach through the hole and observing what happened. Dr. Beaumont discovered much of what we now know about digestion. ■

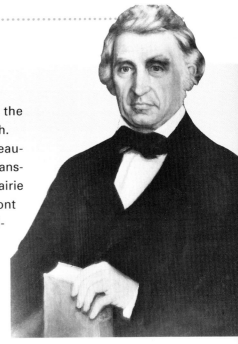

Prairie du Chien is quite small—only about 6,000 people—which belies its importance in Wisconsin history. Although its name is often translated as "prairie dog," it really means "prairie of Big Dog." Big Dog was the chief of an important Native American village at the mouth of the Wisconsin River.

European people began to settle at Prairie du Chien in 1781. Wisconsin's first millionaire was Prairie du Chien's Hercules Dousman, who built the mansion called Villa Louis. Dousman's house was built on the site of Fort Crawford.

CHAPTER SEVEN

Governing the People

I t took two attempts, but the people of Wisconsin approved a constitution in 1848, carving a new state out of the old Northwest Territory. Since that time, the constitution has been amended 132 times but has never been rewritten. The first Wisconsinites did well.

Milwaukee County Courthouse and Douglas MacArthur Square

The Structure of Government

Wisconsin has executive, legislative (or law-making), and judicial branches of government. Six state officials of the executive branch are elected by the people of the state. They are the governor, lieutenant governor, secretary of state, state treasurer, attorney general, and state superintendent of public assistance. They are each elected for four-year terms.

The legislature is divided into the assembly and the senate. People elected to the state assembly serve two-year terms. Senators serve for four years.

The state court system was overhauled in 1977 to simplify the system and to eliminate overlapping functions. In the original state constitution, the supreme court was composed of only three justices. Since then the number has gradually risen to seven. Wisconsin Supreme Court justices are elected for a period of ten years.

Opposite: Students from the University of Wisconsin at Madison

Wisconsin's Governors

Name	Party	Term	Name	Party	Term
Nelson Dewey	Dem.	1848–1852	Francis E. McGovern	Rep.	1911–1915
Leonard J. Farwell	Whig	1852–1854	Emanuel L. Philipp	Rep.	1915–1921
William A. Barstow	Dem.	1854–1856	John J. Blaine	Rep.	1921–1927
Arthur MacArthur	Dem.	1856	Fred R. Zimmerman	Rep.	1927–1929
Coles Bashford	Rep.	1856–1858	Walter J. Kohler Sr.	Rep.	1929–1931
Alexander W. Randall	Rep.	1858–1862	Philip F. La Follette	Rep.	1931–1933
Louis P. Harvey	Rep.	1862	Albert G. Schmedeman	Dem.	1933–1935
Edward Salomon	Rep.	1862–1864	Philip F. La Follette	Prog.	1935–1939
James T. Lewis	Rep.	1864–1866	Julius P. Heil	Rep.	1939–1943
Lucius Fairchild	Rep.	1866–1872	Walter S. Goodland	Rep.	1943–1947
Cadwallader C. Washburn	Rep.	1872–1874	Oscar Rennebohm	Rep.	1947–1951
William R. Taylor	Dem.	1874–1876	Walter J. Kohler Jr.	Rep.	1951–1957
Harrison Ludington	Rep.	1876–1878	Vernon W. Thomson	Rep.	1957–1959
William E. Smith	Rep.	1878–1882	Gaylord A. Nelson	Dem.	1959–1963
Jeremiah McLain Rusk	Rep.	1882–1889	John W. Reynolds	Dem.	1963–1965
William D. Hoard	Rep.	1889–1891	Warren P. Knowles	Rep.	1965–1971
George W. Peck	Dem.	1891–1895	Patrick J. Lucey	Dem.	1971–1977
William H. Upham	Rep.	1895–1897	Martin J. Schreiber	Dem.	1977–1979
Edward Scofield	Rep.	1897–1901	Lee S. Dreyfus	Rep.	1979–1983
Robert M. La Follette Sr.	Rep.	1901–1906	Anthony S. Earl	Dem.	1983–1987
James O. Davidson	Rep.	1906–1911	Tommy G. Thompson	Rep.	1987–

The court of appeals did not exist until the 1977 constitution revision. It divides the state into four different districts for hearing cases that are appealed from lower courts. When the original decision in a case is questionable, people may appeal the case, or ask that it be heard again. Appeals judges are elected for six-year terms.

There are sixty-nine judicial circuits. These are the basic trial courts, where both civil and criminal cases are heard. For the most part, each circuit court covers a full county. A few circuits encompass two counties. Circuit court judges are elected for six-year terms.

Wisconsin's counties

Wisconsin has seventy-two counties. The largest county by size is Marathon with 1,545 square miles (4,002 sq. km). The smallest is Ozaukee with 232 square miles (601 sq km). The largest county by population is Milwaukee; the smallest is Menominee.

The Capital

The first capital of Wisconsin Territory was Belmont, not far from Prairie du Chien. James Duane Doty, a land speculator, and some

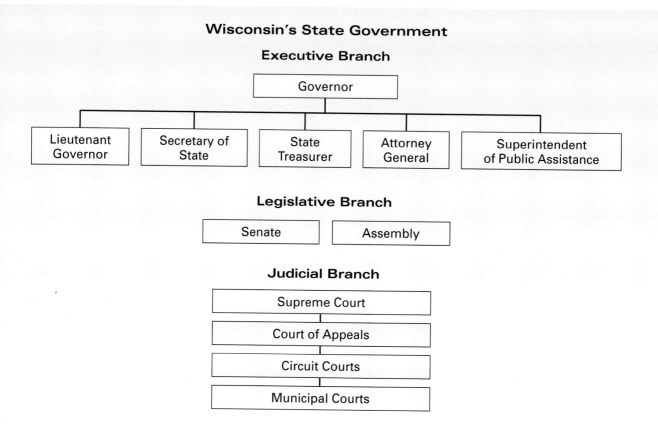

Wisconsin's State Government

Executive Branch

Governor

Lieutenant Governor | Secretary of State | State Treasurer | Attorney General | Superintendent of Public Assistance

Legislative Branch

Senate | Assembly

Judicial Branch

Supreme Court

Court of Appeals

Circuit Courts

Municipal Courts

friends purchased land in the south-central part of Wisconsin Territory. Doty and his friends were determined to make sure that their land became the capital when Wisconsin became a state. Doty gave the site the name of Madison, after President James Madison. He also chose the county's name—Dane—for Nathan Dane, one of the developers of the Northwest Ordinance of 1787.

The public was shocked that the slender but swampy bridge of land connecting the lakes (an isthmus) should be chosen as the new capital. Doty himself became the second territorial governor.

The territorial capitol at Madison, such as it was, was ready in 1838. It was a red-brick building that was already too small before it was even finished. It was certainly too small by the time Wisconsin became a state in 1848. The government officials worked in terrible conditions until a new building could be finished, although construction was interrupted by the Civil War. The capitol was enlarged in the 1880s.

The "New" Capitol

Early in the morning on February 27, 1904, the capitol caught fire. Fire engines were brought by train, too late to save the capitol. The building was beyond repair, though much of the library and the state records were rescued.

The state capitol in Madison

It was thirteen years before a new building was finished. Designed by George B. Post of New York, it was constructed of marble and granite from all over the world. The building has four identical entrances, so one can't really say which is the "front door." The dome of the capitol, which stands almost 300 feet (91 m) high, often serves as a landmark for people within Madison. New Hampshire-born sculptor Daniel Chester French sculpted the female figure, called *Wisconsin,* which stands on top of the dome. Artist Edwin Howland Blashfield painted the huge murals inside the dome and in the assembly chamber.

The assembly was the first government body in the world to use electric voting machines. They were installed in 1917, as the new building went into use.

In recent years, the state offices have spread far and wide throughout the city of Madison because the capitol itself is far too small to accommodate all the employees in the modern government. During the 1990s, the capitol was completely restored.

Capital Park, around the capitol, is the site of a widely attended Farmers' Market. Every Saturday from May to November, farmers and gardeners from all around the area sell their produce there. Art on the Square is an art fair held each year and attended by many thousands of enthusiasts.

Farmers market their wares.

The Wisconsin Idea

Like all states, Wisconsin sends two senators to Washington, D.C. It has nine members in the U.S. House of Representatives. Both the state's representatives in Washington and the government in Madison have made important decisions that have affected the entire nation. Many of these pioneering ideas are part of what came to be called the Wisconsin Idea.

The Wisconsin Idea and the Progressive movement arose because during the last two decades of the nineteenth century, Wisconsin had been controlled by the wealth and power of the railway and timber barons. Many people thought it was time for reform. The leader of Wisconsin's Progressive movement was Robert M. "Fighting Bob" La Follette, who wanted to make government "a servant, not ruler, of people."

"Fighting Bob" La Follette

Robert Marion La Follette was born in Primrose in Dane County in 1855. A lawyer himself, he also married a lawyer—Belle Case, the first woman to receive a law degree from the University of Wisconsin. La Follette, who had previously been a congressman, was elected governor in 1900. Among the legislation he backed was a plan to fix the railway rates so that they would not vary depending on how friendly a shipper was with the railway owners. He also arranged to protect what remained of the state's forests. His new civil service act required that people with government jobs be paid according to their merit, rather than because of their friendships. Such ideas were called "progressive," and when La Follette was sent to Washington, D.C., in 1905, he introduced a number of similarly progressive ideas for the nation. Some people never forgave him for opposing the country's involvement in World War I. However, that didn't keep him from being reelected in 1922.

Two years later, "Fighting Bob" ran as an independent for the office of president of the United States. People all over the country voted for him, giving him 17 percent of the vote. ■

The Progressive Republican Party won control of state government in 1903. With advisers from the University of Wisconsin, the politicians and educators developed laws that would keep children out of factories, ensure that factories were as safe as possible, and make employers pay when workers were injured on the job. The new laws also stipulated that farmers should not have to pay more for shipping goods than other businesspeople paid.

One of "Fighting Bob's" initial reforms established the nation's first statewide direct-primary election system. For the first time, the people of a state had a role in deciding who would appear on the actual ballot in November. As a result of the direct primary, old-time party bosses—usually the wealthiest men in the state who did

The Science Hall at the University of Wisconsin

A Life-Saving Speech

During the presidential campaign of 1912, Theodore "Teddy" Roosevelt, running for the third-party Progressive ticket, came to Milwaukee to give a speech. The talkative man had been speaking for some time when John Schrank, a bartender, fired his .38 caliber revolver at the large former president. The bullet struck a thick copy of Roosevelt's speech and a metal eyeglass case in his vest pocket. It did little damage to the big man's chest. Roosevelt checked the damage and finished his speech before allowing himself to be taken to a hospital. ■

not want to see their businesses hurt by lawmakers—lost control of politics.

Another "idea" was that manufacturers should pay taxes. In 1911, Wisconsin became the first state to collect taxes from manufacturing firms. It also came up with the idea of worker's compensation, which provided that workers who are injured on the job continue to be paid. Before that, a worker was assumed to be working at his own risk. Today, all states have such laws.

President Theodore Roosevelt called Wisconsin "a pioneer blazing the way." Part of the Wisconsin Idea called for professors at the university (which is located only blocks away from the capitol in Madison) to work closely with the people of the state. The entire state would be the university's campus. Many of the state's progressive ideas were drafted by professors at the university.

Wisconsin Women

Carrie Chapman Catt was at the center of the fight for women's right to vote, called suffrage. Born Carrie Lane on a farm near Ripon in 1859, she grew up certain that she could do everything as well as the boys could. She refused to listen when people said, "Girls don't do that!" Before marrying her second husband, George William Catt, she made him agree—in writing—that she could spend four months each year trying to get the vote for women. After his death in 1905, she had both the time and money to spend on woman suffrage. She moved to New York and became a close friend of Susan B. Anthony. She succeeded Anthony as president of the suffrage association.

In 1919, Carrie Chapman Catt succeeded in her mission. The U.S. Congress voted for a constitutional amendment that gave women the right to vote. Fourteen months later, enough states had

Carrie Chapman Catt

She Got It There First

Ada James of Richland Center belonged to a family that believed women had just as much right and ability to vote as men had. When Congress passed the Nineteenth Amendment, her family was influential in getting it voted on in Wisconsin right away. Wisconsin's assembly vote was quite close, 54 to 52, but the senate had only one vote against it.

When James heard by telegraph that Illinois had also ratified the amendment quickly, she and her male relatives urged Governor Emanuel Philipp to appoint James's father as a special messenger. They wanted him to get to Washington, D.C., before the U.S. Post Office's Special Delivery could deliver the Illinois vote. Mr. James traveled day and night, and he made it. Wisconsin went on the record as the first state to ratify the Nineteenth Amendment. ■

Shirley S. Abrahamson

approved, or ratified, the Nineteenth Amendment, so that women could vote.

The first three women to serve in Wisconsin's assembly were elected in 1924, but only one was reelected the following term. A woman wasn't sent to the senate until 1974, when Kathryn Morrison of Platteville was elected. Shirley S. Abrahamson was appointed in 1976 as the first woman to serve on the state supreme court. Abrahamson later became chief justice of the Wisconsin Supreme Court in a statewide election in 1996.

Wisconsin's State Symbols

State motto: "Forward" Sometimes the statue of the woman on the top of the capitol dome is called "Miss Forward" but her official name is *Wisconsin.*

State animal: Badger The badger (top left) was made the official state animal in 1957. Its likeness already appeared on the state seal, flag, and in the capitol architecture, and the animal mentioned in the state song.

State wildlife animal: White-tailed deer The northern counties of Wisconsin campaigned vigorously to make the white-tailed deer the state animal. As a compromise in 1957, it was named the state wildlife animal.

State fish: Muskellunge Members of the Wisconsin legislature attempted to make the "muskie" the state fish as early as 1939. The trout was a very distant alternative suggestion. The designation of the muskie was made official in 1955.

State bird: Robin In 1926–1927, Wisconsin's schoolchildren selected the robin (bottom left) as the state bird. The robin received twice as many votes as any other bird.

State tree: Sugar maple Schoolchildren in 1893, and again in 1948, voted the sugar maple as their favorite tree. The state legislature agreed with the children by making it official in 1949.

State flower: Wood violet In 1908, Wisconsin's schoolchildren nominated four candidates for state flower: the violet, wild rose, trailing arbutus, and white water lily. The final vote was taken on Arbor Day that year, and the violet won. The Wisconsin legislature made the vote law in 1949.

State insect: Honeybee A third-grade class at Holy Family School in Marinette requested that the honeybee be named the state insect. The legislature agreed in 1977.

State rock: Red granite Red granite is mined in several parts of the state and is an igneous rock composed of quartz and feldspar. It was named state rock in 1971 because of its economic importance to the state.

State mineral: Galena A law was passed by the legislature in 1971 naming galena (lead ore) as the state's official mineral.

State fossil: Trilobite Trilobites are a common and easily found and recognized fossil in Wisconsin. The legislature named the trilobite the state fossil in 1985.

State grain: Corn The legislature named corn as the state grain to draw attention to the crop's importance as both a cash crop and as feed for the state's dairy herds. The designation was made in 1989.

State dog: American water spaniel The efforts of schoolchildren to name the American water spaniel the state dog paid off in 1985.

State domesticated animal: Dairy cow The category of "domesticated animal" was added to the list of state symbols in 1971 in recognition of the importance of the dairy cow to the state's economy.

State beverage: Milk Wisconsin was the nation's leading milk-producing state. The designation of milk as the state beverage in 1987 acknowledges that fact.

State soil: Antigo silt loam A state soil was designated in 1983 to remind Wisconsinites of their responsibilities to the land. It took 10,000 years for the productive, rich Antigo silt loam to be formed. ∎

The Wisconsin State Flag

The state flag, adopted in 1913, bears the state seal, name, and year of statehood. The seal contains a badger and symbols of industry and agriculture.

Wisconsin's State Song

Music by William T. Purdy
On, Wisconsin! On, Wisconsin!
Grand old badger state!
We, thy loyal sons and daughters,
Hail thee, good and great.
On, Wisconsin! On, Wisconsin!
Champion of the right,
"Forward," our motto—
God will give thee might!

CHAPTER EIGHT

Bullets, Beer, and Visitors

European people first came to Wisconsin to take advantage of the abundance of fur-bearing animals. The people in Canada and the eastern colonies had established markets to sell furs to European manufacturers. Fortunately, just about the time the wildlife ran out, valuable mineral resources were found in Wisconsin.

Mining for Minerals

The early mining area of Wisconsin was centered at Mineral Point, which was founded in 1827 when deposits of galena, or lead ore, were located by a prospector. Both bullets and paint were made from lead at that time, so it was always in demand. Word of the discovery spread quickly to Cornwall, the jutting southwest corner of England, where mines were beginning to run out of reachable ore. Cornish miners were among the first immigrants to the Wisconsin area.

At first, while lead-mining was growing rapidly in Wisconsin, farmers were not permitted to settle in the lead region except in areas declared free of the valuable ore. When lead prices fell and food prices rose, however, the government opened southwestern Wisconsin Territory to settlement. Wisconsin was not a mineral state again until the 1880s, when a small deposit of iron was found in the Superior region, near Minnesota's mines.

Geologists from the Exxon Corporation discovered zinc-sulfide and copper deposits in Forest County in 1975. The deposits are next to the Sakaogon (Mole Lake) Indian Reservation and the headwaters of the Wolf River. Many people opposed the plan to mine the minerals, and the company dropped its plans until 1994.

Opposite: The Miller Brewing Company

The mine Exxon now wants to open would be huge, with a shaft about 2,600 feet (792 m) deep. Although the mine would provide work for many people and the nation's industry with much-needed copper, the process of mining creates acidic waste that would be dumped in the Wolf River. The battle between Exxon and environmentalists could go on for many years.

Agriculture and Dairy Production

In its early days, Wisconsin was a major source of wheat for the entire country, and flour-milling was an important business. In 1842, J. I. Case of Milwaukee moved into the Racine area, bringing with him a number of wheat-threshing machines. A few years later, he started his own factory, making important improvements in the design of threshers, which soon sold throughout the country. J. I. Case remains a major industry today, but Wisconsin lost status

Holstein cows graze in a fertile valley near Black Earth.

as a wheat-producing state when other states with better growing conditions were settled. The last straw was an invasion of destructive chinch bugs that ruined the Wisconsin wheat crop. More and more farmers reluctantly turned to dairy farming.

Throughout most of the nineteenth century, New York was regarded as the only source for good cheese. That changed when Wisconsin dairy farmers planted an English grass that made the cows produce large quantities of good milk. Then, in 1871, refrigerated railway cars were invented, and it was possible to take cheese and even butter to markets in the East.

Most small farmers could make butter, but it took a major dairy farmer to make cheese in commercial quantities. In 1890, Stephen M. Babcock of the University of Wisconsin in Madison invented the butterfat tester. Until then, a cheese maker could only hope that the milk he was using had a high enough content of fat to make good cheese. Wisconsin soon acquired a reputation for producing the best cheese in the country.

Today, Wisconsin is known for all its dairy products, including milk, cream, butter, and, most of all, cheese. The United States makes more cheese than any other country, and Wisconsin makes more cheese than any other state. Most of the cheeses made are similar to European varieties, but two cheeses, Brick and Colby, were invented in Wisconsin. Today, the center of cheese-making is Monroe County.

Butter as a product was put in peril by the invention of oleomargarine, an "imitation" butter made of vegetable oils instead of milk. For several decades, margarine—which was white—was sold

What Wisconsin Grows, Manufactures, and Mines

Agriculture
Dairy products
Corn
Hay
Beef cattle

Manufacturing
Industrial machinery and equipment
Food and food products
Metal products
Printing and publishing

Mining
Stone
Sand and gravel
Copper
Lime
Lead and zinc

Today, most cheese factories in Wisconsin are automated.

with a small packet of yellow dye that could be mixed in to make the margarine look like butter. Wisconsin, fighting for butter all the way, did not allow the sale of margarine within its boundaries until the 1960s.

Agricultural Notes

The Civil War's demand for meat turned Wisconsin into a major meatpacking state. Dairy farmers usually raised pigs, too, feeding them the milk parts that were not used for drinking or making cheese. One early meat packer was Philip Armour, who made a fortune during the Civil War. He went to Chicago and helped turn that city into the meatpacking center of the United States. Oscar Mayer, on the other hand, moved his sausage-making business from Chicago to Madison, and it is one of the largest meat-product companies in the world today.

The College of Agriculture at the University of Wisconsin was responsible for producing hybrids of sweet corn. Although Wisconsin's summer is shorter than most other corn-growing states, the hybrids develop before autumn sets in. Wisconsin's sweet corn, as well as its green beans and peas, make it one of the biggest states for vegetable canning and freezing.

Wisconsin also grows record-breaking quantities of cranberries, large tobacco leaves for use in wrapping cigars, and ginseng, a root

A cranberry farm in Tomah

used in Asia for medicine. The Japanese firm Kikkoman has a huge soy-sauce factory in Walworth County that takes advantage of the large crops of soybeans grown in southern Wisconsin.

The Woods

The forested landscape of northern Wisconsin changed greatly within just a few short years. Probably the first sawmill in the state was built on Devil's River near De Pere in about 1809. Soon there were many sawmills. However, lumbering was such a small business that the new capitol at Madison had to be built with lumber brought from Pennsylvania.

Frederick Weyerhaeuser, a German immigrant in Rock Island, Illinois, needed trees to keep his big mills busy. In 1864, he discovered the vast forests of Wisconsin's Chippewa Valley. Lumberjacks—many of them immigrants—came by the thousands to cut down the trees. They cut roads through the forests and established logging camps. Some camps evolved into permanent towns when the men brought their wives and children, but most became ghost towns when the lumberjacks moved out.

Cut logs were moved by horse- or oxen-drawn sleds to a hill above the nearest river. There, they were branded for later identification and then slid down the hillside into the water. The logs were fastened together into

Logs being loaded onto a truck

Wisconsin's natural resources

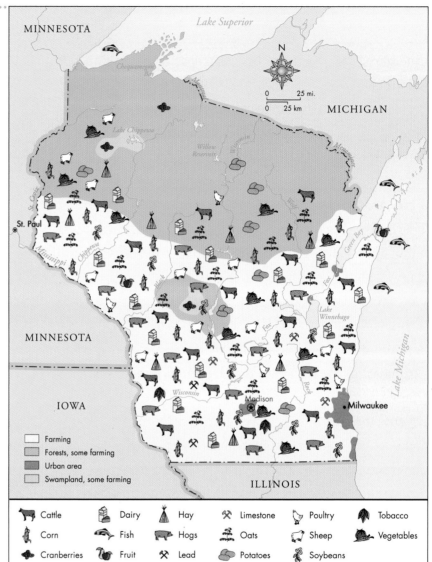

Paper companies in Rhinelander are now replacing the trees they cut down.

Map legend:

- Farming
- Forests, some farming
- Urban area
- Swampland, some farming

Cattle	Dairy	Hay	Limestone	Poultry	Tobacco
Corn	Fish	Hogs	Oats	Sheep	Vegetables
Cranberries	Fruit	Lead	Potatoes	Soybeans	

giant rafts and floated downstream. Their destination was the nearest sawmill. Many northern towns grew up near sawmills. Marinette, Wausau, Chippewa Falls, and Black River Falls are among the towns that flourished. Some of them also suffered because of the mills. Oshkosh, for example, was almost completely destroyed by fire three times in about one year.

For two decades, millions of trees were cut. The stumps and waste were left in place as the lumberjacks moved on. Often, the waste caught fire and thousands of acres burned. The great North

The Peshtigo Fire

On October 8, 1871, the same day the Great Chicago Fire began, the nation's most disastrous forest fire started at Peshtigo in northern Wisconsin. The region had received no rain for many months, and the forests surrounding the lumber town flared instantly. The fire left a blackened and barren area that was 40 miles (64 km) long and 10 miles (16 km) wide. About 1,200 people died in the Peshtigo Fire, 900 more than died in the Chicago Fire. Just one day after the tragic fire, it finally rained in Peshtigo. ◼

Woods became the great barren Cutover. No effort was made to look beyond the end of the tree supply. It wasn't until 1903 that Wisconsin hired its first state forester.

In 1944, an organization called Trees for Tomorrow Natural Resources Education Center began to distribute millions of young trees and to encourage landowners to plant them. The organization's headquarters was the first environmental education center in the United States. Thanks to Trees for Tomorrow, and considerable help from nature, most of the Cutover has regrown.

Carrying on with Paper

Paper has been made in Wisconsin since it became a state, but the paper mills near the dams on the Fox River north of Lake Winnebago were started during the heyday of logging in the Northwoods. When the trees were gone, the paper mills had to find new resources for the chopped-up wood that provides the fiber in paper. For many years, mills bought wood from Canada. Newspapers, who were the biggest users of paper, found that it was less expensive to buy Canadian paper directly. The Wisconsin paper manufacturers turned to making other products, such as tissues. Kimberly-Clark and Fort Howard are among the large paper-product companies.

Unfortunately, the availability of rivers in which to dump the toxic chemicals used in manufacturing was seen as an advantage by Wisconsin paper companies. So, for decades, Wisconsin's rivers were dangerously polluted. Since 1961, a campaign has been underway to get the papermakers to find other, safer ways to dispose of their toxic waste. Today, the waterways are well on their way to being cleaned up. The companies also developed ways to use up to 60 percent less water in the manufacturing process.

Wisconsin paper mills employ many people.

Machines—Onward and Upward

Dairy farms seem to have little to do with heavy machinery, but it is farming that has turned Wisconsin into one of the major providers of machinery. Allis-Chalmers and J. I. Case farm machines were used the world over. Allis-Chalmers is gone now, but Case has merged with International Harvester, and its red machines are seen everywhere.

In 1868, Christopher Latham Sholes, a newspaper editor from Kenosha, received a patent for the typewriter. Sholes sold the rights to the hugely successful machine to the Remington Arms Company, a gun manufacturer, for only $12,000.

One of the most successful early cars was the Rambler, produced in Kenosha by the Thomas B. Jeffery Company in 1902. Charles W. Nash later bought the plant and changed the vehicle's name to Nash. Thirty years later, Nash merged with another automobile manufacturer to form American Motors. Chrysler bought American Motors, and the old plant was closed in 1988. Chrysler still makes Jeep engines in Kenosha.

Four-wheel-drive vehicles (cars that deliver power to all four wheels and can thus move over rough terrain) were invented in Wisconsin. William Besserdich of Clintonville invented the system in 1906 in a car he called the Battleship. Other automakers in

Charles W. Nash

Billy Mitchell Was Right

Milwaukee International Airport (left) is generally called Mitchell Field after General Billy Mitchell, son of a Milwaukee executive. As an officer in the U.S. Army, Mitchell was head of the U.S. fliers who fought over Europe in World War I. That experience convinced him that aviation was the wave of the future. However, even after he demonstrated that a warship could be sunk from the air, the Army disagreed with him. When he publicly criticized his superiors' decisions, he was court-martialed—tried in a military court. Mitchell was forced to resign and did not live to see that he was proved right. When World War II was starting, the Army formed the Army Air Corps, which eventually became the U.S. Air Force. ■

Wisconsin included the Kissels of Hartford. From 1906 to about 1930, they made the Kisselkar and various trucks. Today, General Motors has a large assembly plant at Janesville.

Because the Wisconsin constitution would not allow state funds to be used for roads, Wisconsinites who liked the newfangled cars suffered on the state's roads. The constitution was changed in 1908, but highway construction had to wait until 1917 when a state highway system was planned and started. Wisconsin became the first state in the nation to establish numbered highways to simplify a driver's task of following the right road.

Wisconsin was a pioneering state in aviation, too. Albert W. Lawson of the Milwaukee area established Lawson Air Line in 1919, and Hamilton Aero Manufacturing Company built airplanes until 1930. Hamilton's private airstrip eventually became Milwaukee International Airport. The popular Midwest Express airline headquartered at Milwaukee began as the corporate airline of the Wisconsin paper-products firm of Kimberly-Clark.

Clever Wisconsinites

John Stevens of Neenah invented the roller mill—a device that ground flour better than any previous flour mill had done. Stevens acquired a patent in 1876 for his mill, which used two smooth rollers instead of grooved stones to grind wheat. The Edward P. Allis Company of Milwaukee (later part of Allis-Chalmers) produced a huge rolling mill that put the Washburn Mill of Minneapolis in business as the giant food corporation General Mills.

Warren Johnson, a natural-science professor at Whitewater State College, was annoyed by frequent changes in the temperature of his classroom. In 1885, he invented a device called a "thermostat" to keep the heat level consistent. His thermostat was the first product of the Milwaukee firm, Johnson Electric Service. Today, Johnson Controls, the largest publicly held firm in Wisconsin, is known worldwide.

The story goes that Ole Evinrude thought that it took too long to row a boat across Lake Okauchee when he wanted to impress his fiancée by bringing her ice cream. In 1907, he invented one of the first practical motors that could be mounted on the back of a boat. Evinrude's engines were the first outboard motors.

The Great Chicago Fire of 1871 created many opportunities for Milwaukee. One of them was beer sales. Most of Chicago's breweries burned, and railways that carried ice on refrigerated cars allowed Milwaukee's breweries to start supplying beer all over the

Population of Wisconsin's Major Cities (1990)	
Milwaukee	628,088
Madison	191,262
Green Bay	96,466
Racine	84,298
Kenosha	80,352
Appleton	65,695

The famous Schlitz stables building

Midwest. Schlitz used the slogan, "The Beer that Made Milwaukee Famous." In recent years, Milwaukee has been joined by St. Louis, Missouri, as the center of the beer-making industry.

Seymour Cray of Chippewa Falls designed supercomputers. In 1972, he founded his own company—Cray Research—to make the world's fastest computer, the Cray 1. "I was one of those nerds before the name was popular," said Cray.

Hospitality and Tourism

One of the very first laws written to govern Wisconsin Territory regulated taverns. Among other things, the tavern keeper was required to have at least two spare beds "with sufficient sheeting" for guests. So taverns were the state's earliest inns for visitors.

Fountain Spring House at Waukesha was one of the first tourist hotels. It opened in 1864 on the site of "health-giving" springs. Eventually it became a huge resort that could accommodate 800 guests.

Newhall House in Milwaukee was, for a time, the most luxurious hotel west of New York. Built in 1857, it had 300 rooms on six stories. Abraham Lincoln spoke there in 1859. In 1883, the hotel burned, killing perhaps 160 people. Tom Thumb, known as the "world's smallest human"—he was only 25 inches (63.5 cm) tall—was among the survivors.

The newfangled industry of tourism really got its start after the Chicago Fire of 1871. Some wealthy Chicago families moved up

The Other Kind of "Hog"

As the twentieth century began, two young men in Milwaukee decided that they could make a better motorcycle. By 1903, William Harley and Arthur Davidson had their first model ready to sell. Within a few years, their motorcycles were going 60 miles (97 km) per hour and dominating races around the country. The U.S. Army bought thousands of Harley-Davidson motorcycles for use in both World War I and World War II. Harley-Davidson became the largest motorcycle manufacturer in the world. In 1998, the ninety-fifth anniversary of the company was celebrated by thousands of riders on Harley-Davidsons, popularly called "Hogs," who paraded through the streets of Milwaukee. ■

to southeastern Wisconsin—especially the Lake Geneva area—while the city was rebuilt. Later, with numerous new millionaires developing as the city grew, they built second homes in the same area. Today, Wisconsin is sometimes called "Chicago's playground." On an average summer day, at least half the vacationers are from Illinois, mainly from the Chicago area.

When it was discovered that tourists would come to the Cutover to go fishing even if there were few trees, one newspaper excitedly observed, "We can sell our climate and scenery year after year and still retain it forever." Northern Wisconsin opened its arms to people who were attracted to the thousands of little lakes. Today, there are three primary tourist areas in Wisconsin: the Geneva Lakes area; the North Woods, centered at Minocqua; and Door County.

CHAPTER NINE

The Wisconsin Mix

People from more than fifty nations came to Wisconsin during the height of the immigrant era. Today, even more nationalities are represented in the state, but it was the first fifty that gave Wisconsin the character that it has today.

Milwaukee's annual Summerfest after sunset

In many parts of Wisconsin, descendants of the first settlers show visitors how their people lived by opening their homes and performing at festivals. The celebration of their immigrant heritage is still an important part of the lives of many Wisconsinites.

Festivals and Fairs

Milwaukee can easily be called the City of Festivals. On summer weekends, some of the main immigrant groups that formed Wisconsin are recognized in the eight ethnic festivals held in the city. The Asian Moon Festival and Polish Fest are celebrated in June; Italians and Germans entertain in July; August is the time for African, Irish, and Mexican festivals; and the season ends in September with a large Native American ceremonial and gathering.

Milwaukee's largest celebration is Summerfest, begun in 1968, and among the world's biggest music festivals. For ten days in late June and early July, eleven stages at a lakefront site feature every kind of music, from classical to folk to rhythm and blues.

Not all such entertainment takes place in the cities. County fairs are immensely popular throughout the state. They began in

Opposite: A crowd at Milwaukee's Summerfest

Wisconsin when settlers in the northern areas were living isolated lives. The only way they could learn about new techniques and products was to gather together in one place at the same time. The wonderful county fairs were the best way to do this. Although the Wisconsin State Fair is held in Milwaukee each year, the smaller county fairs remain an enjoyable and educational time for many people.

The Native Americans

According to the Wisconsin State Historical Society, "virtually every experiment in the history of Indian policy has been tried out on one tribe or another in Wisconsin." And this experimentation resulted in the "progressive impoverishment of the Indian peoples." Today, however, the Native Americans are improving their lives. Since gambling has been permitted on Native American land, most Wisconsin tribes have raised their standard of living.

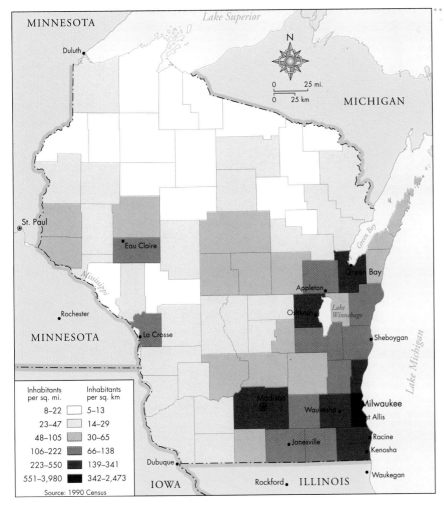

Inhabitants per sq. mi. | Inhabitants per sq. km
8–22 / 5–13
23–47 / 14–29
48–105 / 30–65
106–222 / 66–138
223–550 / 139–341
551–3,980 / 342–2,473
Source: 1990 Census

Wisconsin's population density

Native Americans were the largest minority group in Wisconsin until 1950, when their numbers were surpassed by African-Americans. More than 34,000 Native Americans now live in Wisconsin. More Native Americans live in Milwaukee than on any single Wisconsin reservation. Milwaukee Indian Community School was started by a few mothers who wanted extra attention given to Indian children who were in danger of dropping out of school. An Indian health facility also operates in Milwaukee, built and staffed by Native Americans.

Traditional Native American dance competitions attract various tribes from Wisconsin and out of state.

The Ojibwa moved into the Wisconsin area in historic times as they moved westward in the quest for furs wanted by white traders. There are six Ojibwa reservations in the northern part of the state. However, the lands are not fully owned by the tribes. Instead, they were formed around land owned by people of European descent. Today, these people live in clusters within the reservations.

The Winnebago now call themselves Ho-Chunk, or Hochungara. The Ho-Chunk serve venison at their ritual feasts. Because they have no tribal rights and own no reservations, they had to negotiate the right to hunt deer during the off-season. Today, in addition to the famous Stand Rock Ceremonial, the Ho-Chunk own a major casino at Wisconsin Dells.

Reservations in the state include the Menominee and the Potawatomi. The Potawatomi reservations are on scattered lands in Forest, Oconto, and Wood counties. In 1856, the Menominee gave

Lillie Rosa Minoka-Hill

Lillie Rosa Minoka was the daughter of a Mohawk woman and a Quaker physician in Philadelphia in the 1880s. After her mother's death, Lillie was raised by her father's family. She became a doctor, graduating from the Women's Medical College of Pennsylvania in 1899.

On marrying Charles Hill in 1905, Lillie Rosa Minoka-Hill moved to Oneida, Wisconsin. Although she had intended to be a mother and help her husband with his farming, she gradually found herself doctoring the community with both Western medicine and Native American treatments. However, she was unable to admit patients to hospitals or be reimbursed by the government for spending money on medicines. After years of serving unofficially, in 1934 she finally took and passed the exam to be licensed by the state of Wisconsin. Minoka-Hill was adopted by the Oneida tribe and given the Indian name "She Who Serves." ∎

Yellow Thunder

In 1837, a number of Native Americans from the Winnebago, or Ho-Chunk, tribe went to Washington, D.C., where they signed a treaty with the U.S. government. The government did not keep the promises made in this treaty. Just three years later, the government tried to move the Winnebago west of the Mississippi. Some members of the tribe moved and became the Winnebago tribe that now lives in Nebraska. Other tribe members led by Yellow Thunder kept returning to Wisconsin.

Yellow Thunder understood the government's idea of owning land, even though it was contrary to Native American tradition. He and his people began to buy 40-acre (16-ha) plots throughout the state of Wisconsin. In the 1870s, more Winnebago were forced to move west. Again, they returned to Wisconsin. Finally, the government allowed them to settle down on their own plots of land. As land-owners, they could no longer be forced to leave. Unlike many other tribes, the Winnebago have no reservation in Wisconsin.

Today, Yellow Thunder's people are officially recognized as the Wisconsin Winnebago Nation. ■

the Stockbridge-Munsee Tribal Council land for a reservation. They were from New York of Mahican (or Mohican) origin. The Oneida, also from New York, were of Iroquois origin. They gave their name to Oneida County in the northern part of the state, but their reservation is southwest of Green Bay.

Education

Schools were established in Wisconsin in 1816, when the children of soldiers stationed at the forts at Green Bay, Portage, and Prairie du Chien began attending classes. In the early 1800s, children were not expected to spend much time in school. When the University of Wisconsin was founded in 1849, there was only one public high school in the entire state. The others were church-related academies.

In the nineteenth century, some educators became convinced that children could learn a lot more if they started early with organized play that helped them learn. Called *kindergarten,* which is German for "garden of children," the concept was started in America by Margarethe Meyer Schurz of Watertown in 1856. She opened a kindergarten for the benefit of her own daughter and other young relatives.

Milwaukee, where the majority of African-Americans in Wisconsin now live, was slow to integrate public schools. It was the low quality of the mostly black schools that brought about the state's school-voucher plan in 1990. Under this plan, a student in a low-income Milwaukee family could use the funds allotted for one child's education to attend a private school. Though there was no real improvement in test scores achieved by black students in the first few years of the program, many children stayed in school who might otherwise have dropped out. Other states are also investigating "school choice."

Higher Education

The oldest institution of higher learning in Wisconsin is Nashotah House, an Episcopal seminary that was founded in 1841 as an Indian mission and a seminary. It is still open today. Carroll College in nearby Waukesha, chartered in 1846, is the oldest private college in Wisconsin.

Lawrence University in Appleton was coeducational from the time it opened its doors in 1847. (The University of Wisconsin did not turn coed until the Civil War, when there were not enough male students to keep it going.) Catherine Beecher, sister of writer

Harriet Beecher Stowe, was instrumental in the 1850s in changing the small Milwaukee Female Seminary into what became Milwaukee-Downer College. In the late twentieth century, Milwaukee-Downer sold its campus to the University of Wisconsin–Milwaukee and merged with Lawrence.

One of the top-rated public universities in the country, the University of Wisconsin is a huge system that covers the entire state, though when people talk about "the university," they usually mean the school at Madison.

The other universities in the system grew out of the state's commitment to training teachers at many locations. The schools were first called "normal," which meant they trained elementary-school teachers, and then became known as State Teachers' Colleges. In 1971, the teachers' colleges and the university merged. There are campuses at Milwaukee, Eau Claire, Green Bay, La Crosse, Oshkosh, Kenosha (called Parkside), Platteville, River Falls, Stevens Point, Menomonie (called Stout), Superior, and Whitewater. The total system has more than 100,000 students.

In addition, the state has sixteen technical colleges. This system grew out of apprenticeship programs, in which students went to high school part-time and worked part-time in order to learn a job. In 1911, Wisconsin became the first state to establish a statewide system of support for vocational and technical schools.

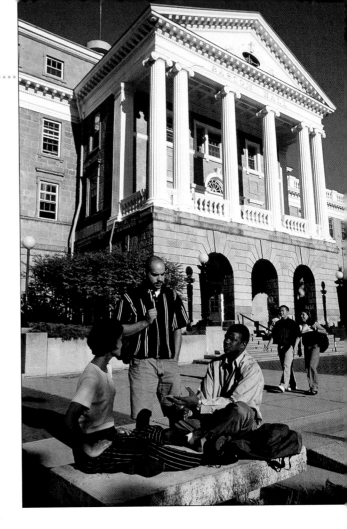

The University of Wisconsin at Madison

CHAPTER TEN

Painters and Packers

n 1846, even before Wisconsin became a state, the Historical Society of Wisconsin was founded as a private organization. In 1853, it was given official responsibility for the preservation of records and other materials of historical interest to the state. It is the oldest state historical society in the nation.

Since 1977, the State Historical Society of Wisconsin has also been responsible for preserving historic sites. It maintains the first capitol in Belmont, Madeline Island Historical Museum, and Old Wade House—a stagecoach inn built in 1851 near Sheboygan.

This thirteen-sided barn, located near Elkhart Lake, was built in 1915.

Three historic locations are found in the southwest corner of the state. Pendarvis, a collection of Cornish miners' houses, is in Mineral Point on Shake Rag Street. It was given that name because women in the houses would shake a cloth out the door to tell their miner husbands that dinner was ready. Not far away on the Mississippi at Prairie du Chien is Villa Louis, the mansion of fur trader Hercules Dousman, the state's first millionaire. At Cassville on the river, the society runs Stonefield Village, a reconstructed village on land once owned by Nelson Dewey, the first governor.

The State Historical Society of Wisconsin is also creating Old World Wisconsin, an outdoor museum at Eagle. Homes and other well-preserved buildings representing various eras and ethnic groups have been moved there. People in costumes of the period tell visitors what life was like at the time the building was used.

Opposite: A portrait of the famous Mona Lisa painted on the side of a Wisconsin barn

Frank Lloyd Wright

The most famous American architect of the twentieth century was Wisconsinite Frank Lloyd Wright. Born in Richland Center in 1867, he became the main architect of what is called the Prairie School of Architecture, meaning that the buildings were supposed to reflect the flat, horizontal look of the Midwestern prairies.

Wright's primary business was in the Chicago area, but near Spring Green he built Taliesin (above), a home named for a Welsh poet, which also housed a school for architects. The house, which has a huge tree growing through the living room, has been described as "embracing the environment." It burned to the ground in 1914 when Wright's cook went crazy and murdered several people. Wright rebuilt the house, which is still visited by thousands of people every year.

Wright gained fame in 1923 when the Imperial Hotel he designed for Tokyo, Japan, was the only large building left standing after a terrible earthquake. The headquarters of S. C. Johnson and Son Company in Racine is one of the most important office buildings designed by Wright. ■

Scribblers and Sculptors

Among the first women artists to become nationally famous was Wisconsinite Vinnie Ream, born in Madison in 1847. Ream discovered the pleasures of sculpting when she watched a statue being made at the capitol. Later, because her father was a government official, she had the opportunity to sculpt the busts (head and shoulders) of many people in Congress. She was still working on the figure of President Lincoln when he was assassinated. Though only eighteen, she was given a contract to do a full figure of Lincoln, which stands in the Capitol in Washington, D.C.

Probably the most famous woman painter of recent decades has been Georgia O'Keeffe. Best known for her huge close-ups of flowers and scenes of the Southwest desert, she was born in Sun Prairie in 1887.

Laura Ingalls was born in a cabin near Pepin in 1867. At sixteen, she became a teacher and then married neighbor Alonzo Wilder. She did not start writing the famed *Little House* series of books about growing up in pioneer days until she was sixty-five years old. Her first book, *Little House in the Big Woods,* tells about her Wisconsin childhood.

Laura Ingalls Wilder

Several Wisconsin-born writers have won Pulitzer Prizes— annual awards given for novels, plays, poetry, and journalism. Thornton Wilder (no relative of Laura Ingalls) was born in Madison. He won Pulitzers for the novel *The Bridge of San Luis Rey* and two Broadway plays, *Our Town* and *The Skin of Our Teeth.* Zona Gale, a native of Portage, won the 1921 Pulitzer Prize for her play about small-town life, *Miss Lulu Bett.*

The Circus State

Circuses were popular and plentiful in Wisconsin even before it became a state. In 1847, the Mabie Brothers Circus was heading toward Janesville when the brothers saw Delavan and decided to stay. They bought land for their permanent quarters, and soon circus people from all over the country converged on small-town Delavan.

Many other would-be circus owners came to Delavan, hoping to find people to employ. In 1870, two people joined the great showman P. T. Barnum in forming a circus in Delavan. In all,

The historic Ringling Theater (above left) in Baraboo

Each year, thousands of visitors flock to the Circus World Museum in Baraboo (above right).

almost thirty different circuses were formed in Delavan, Wisconsin's Circus City.

Seven boys in the August Rüngeling family of Iowa and Prairie du Chien grew up entertaining themselves. These boys (who Americanized their name to Ringling) eventually started putting on shows for other people. The first one was held at Mazomanie, near Madison, in 1882. That show was indoors, but soon they went to Baraboo, where they performed in a huge tent that would hold many people. Eventually they merged their show with the biggest circus on the East Coast, the Barnum & Bailey Circus, which had grown out of Delavan's P. T. Barnum Circus. The resulting circus was known as the "Greatest Show on Earth."

After a terrible 1944 tent fire that killed 168 people, the Greatest Show on Earth moved indoors. The Circus World Museum at Baraboo, however, continues to put on a small but exciting tent show each day for visitors to the Wisconsin Dells area.

Many of the beautiful wagons used by circuses in the past have long since disappeared, but a great collection is on exhibit at Circus World Museum. Each year, these colorful reminders of America's past are put on railway cars and taken to Milwaukee. Once again, thousands come to watch the Great Circus Parade of 600 horses, more than 70 antique circus wagons, and more than 100 clowns.

Professional Teams

Wisconsin may be smaller than many states that support professional sporting teams, but that doesn't stop it from being right up there in the big leagues.

The Green Bay Packers professional football team was organized by Curly (Earl Louis) Lambeau in 1919. It was sponsored by the Acme Meat Packing Company, which gave it the nickname "Packers." The support of one company was not enough, however,

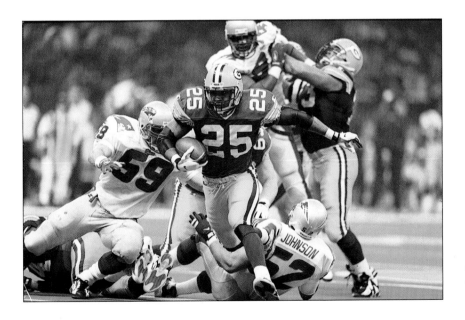

To Fall or Not to Fall

Drivers on the rivers had to be able to stay erect on the logs they were taking downstream, so they learned to birl—to keep their feet moving as the logs rolled in the water. Birling is a contest between two men on one log, spinning the log faster and faster, or even stopping abruptly, to see who can remain standing longest. It's not just a male occupation, though. Mary Jean Malotte of Cornell became a World Champion in the 1930s and paid her way through college with her earnings. Birling is just one of the contests in the World Lumberjack Championships held at Hayward each year. ■

In 1997, the Green Bay Packers won a victory over New England at Super Bowl XXXI in New Orleans.

The Super Coach

New Yorker Vince Lombardi coached the New York Giants before being asked in 1959 to do something about the always-losing Green Bay Packers team. In almost no time, the Packer players were taking themselves and Lombardi seriously. They began to win, and were ready to take the crown when the National Football League and the short-lived American Football League began the annual Super Bowl Championship Games in 1967. They won their first two Super Bowls. Lombardi appeared on a U.S. postage stamp in 1997. ■

and in 1926, shares in the ownership of the team were sold to the citizens of Green Bay.

The Green Bay Packers play at Lambeau Field. In 1967 and 1968, with Vince Lombardi as coach, the Packers won the first two Super Bowl games. The fabled Packers of the 1960s are considered among the greatest teams in any sport in any era. But through the 1970s and 1980s, the Packers met only moderate success. Today, however, with superstar quarterback Brett Favre at the helm, the Pack is back. They crushed the league in 1996, winning Super Bowl XXXI on January 28, 1997. Favre led his team back to the championship game the next year, but the champions were unseated by Denver.

There may not be another American sports team with as devoted a following as the Green Bay Packers. Thousands of fans from around the state flock to Packer games. There is never an empty seat to be found—even on December days with temperatures below zero! Packer fans think of themselves as one big family, some affectionately calling themselves "cheeseheads" because they wear big foam-rubber wedges of Swiss cheese on their heads. Wisconsin sports fans are famous for inventing "tailgate parties." On the day of the game they arrive a couple of hours before kickoff, open up the trunks of their cars and vans, grill some bratwurst on the barbecue, and have a wonderful (if chilly) picnic in the stadium parking lot.

For decades, football was the only big-time sport played in Wisconsin. But in 1953, baseball came to town. After more than seven decades in Boston, the Braves moved to Milwaukee in the spring of 1953, setting up shop in the brand-new County Stadium. Within

Bud Selig

Allan "Bud" Selig is the long-time owner of the Milwaukee Brewers. In recent years, however, he has taken on a much greater role in the world of baseball.

Major League Baseball has traditionally been governed by a commissioner, but in 1992, Commissioner Fay Vincent was fired and no replacement has yet been named.

Bud Selig, as chairman of the game's Executive Council, became "temporary commissioner," and has held the sometimes-uncomfortable position ever since. Selig was at the controls through baseball's worst nightmare: the 1994 labor dispute that lasted 232 days and led to the cancellation of the World Series for the first time in history.

Today, Selig is leading the game out of that dark period and into happier times. ■

four years, the team defeated the mighty New York Yankees in the 1957 World Series. Despite the presence of the Braves' superstar, slugger Henry "Hammerin' Hank" Aaron, local support for the team soon dwindled, and the team moved to Atlanta in 1966. Hank Aaron went with them, and in Atlanta he eventually broke baseball's most coveted record: Babe Ruth's lifetime home-run total of 714. But baseball returned to Wisconsin with the birth of the Milwaukee Brewers in 1972. Brewers fans' biggest thrill came in 1982, when the team won the American League pennant before falling in the World Series to the St. Louis Cardinals.

In 1997, work began on a new stadium for the Brewers in Milwaukee. To be called Miller Park, it will seat 42,500 people and have a convertible roof. It will have the look of an old-time ball park on the outside.

Milwaukee was awarded a National Basketball Association (NBA) franchise in 1968. Success came quickly to the new Milwaukee Bucks as they took the NBA championship in 1971, led by their incredible center Lew Alcindor, who later changed his name to Kareem Abdul-Jabbar. The Bucks just about collapsed when Abdul-

Jabbar was traded to the Los Angeles Lakers. Today they are a competitive team led by forward Glenn Robinson.

The University of Wisconsin's teams in Madison are called the Badgers. They play in the Big Ten Conference. In 1995, the Badgers went to the Rose Bowl in California and won this most coveted of football's bowl games. It had been thirty-four years since Wisconsin had gone to the Rose Bowl.

A Badgers football game at Camp Randall Stadium

Sports in the Cold

The Scots brought the sport of curling to Wisconsin. In those days, the game was played on frozen rivers. One person on the team slides a heavy stone along the ice, hoping that it will stop in a good place to win points. A teammate runs ahead of the stone, sweeping the ice to make it smooth and clean. Today, competitions are held on indoor curling rinks.

Skiing was brought to Wisconsin by the Norwegians about 1880. Because of its lack of high mountains, Wisconsin is not a great downhill-skiing state, but its beautiful North Woods offer wonderful cross-country skiing. The Birkebeiner is a 55-kilometer cross-country ski race that is held each year in the Cable area near Hayward. The name means "birch legs" in Norwegian. More than

7,000 skiers participate, making it one of the biggest cross-country ski races in the world.

There are probably as many as 350 cross-country skiing facilities throughout the state. They vary from small urban parks to well-maintained trails through national forests. The same kind of countryside, as well as the thousands of frozen lakes, makes snowmobiling a popular sport.

As might be expected of a cold northern state, ice skating is very popular in Wisconsin. The Heiden family of Madison is proof. Eric Heiden won five gold medals, the most ever in individual events, at the 1980 Winter Olympics at Lake Placid, New York. Eric's sister Beth could not participate in the Olympics, but she had previously won all four races at the 1979 World Speed Skating Championships.

Eric Heiden skating at the Olympics

In 1992, a gift was given to Wisconsin skaters at all levels of ability. Lloyd and Jane Bradley Pettit, who had previously donated Milwaukee's Bradley Center, opened the Pettit National Ice Center in West Allis. One of only three great speed-skating arenas in the world, it is the official Olympic speed-skating training site. At the 1994 Winter Olympics, at Lillehammer, Norway, Dan Jansen of West Allis showed the value of the Pettit arena when he won the 1,000-meter speed-skating race and set a world record. Illinois's Bonnie Blair, who took two gold medals, also trained at the Pettit Center.

Timeline

United States History

1607 The first permanent British settlement is established in North America at Jamestown.

1620 Pilgrims found Plymouth Colony, the second permanent British settlement.

1776 America declares its independence from England.

1783 The Treaty of Paris officially ends the Revolutionary War in America.

1787 U.S. Constitution is written.

1803 Louisiana Purchase almost doubles the size of the United States.

1812–15 U.S and Britain fight the War of 1812.

1861–65 The North and South fight each other in the American Civil War.

Wisconsin State History

1634 French explorer Jean Nicolet becomes the first European in the area.

1673 Louis Jolliet and Jacques Marquette reach the Mississippi River.

1717 The first permanent European settlement in Wisconsin is established.

1763 France cedes all territories east of the Mississippi River.

1783 Great Britain cedes the area including Wisconsin to the United States.

1822 Lead mining begins in Wisconsin.

1832 The Black Hawk War ends Native American resistance to settlers in Wisconsin.

1836 Madison is made territorial capital.

1848 Wisconsin becomes thirtieth state to join the Union.

1854 Republican Party is founded in Wisconsin.

United States History

The United States is **1917-18** involved in World War I.

Stock market crashes, plunging the **1929** United States into the Great Depression.

The United States fights in **1941-45** World War II.

The United States becomes a **1945** charter member of the United Nations.

The United States fights **1951-53** in the Korean War.

The U.S. Congress enacts a series of **1964** ground-breaking civil rights laws.

The United States **1964-73** engages in the Vietnam War.

The United States and other **1991** nations fight the brief Gulf War against Iraq.

Wisconsin State History

1871 Twelve hundred people die in tragic Peshtigo forest fire.

1890 Stephen M. Babcock develops a machine to test the amount of butterfat in milk, boosting dairy production.

1900 Robert M. La Follette is elected governor and brings wide-ranging reforms.

1910 Victor Berger of Milwaukee becomes the first Socialist elected to the U.S. Congress.

1911 State income tax is enacted.

1932 The nation's first unemployment compensation law is enacted in Wisconsin.

1959 St. Lawrence Seaway opens, bringing benefits to Wisconsin's ports.

1971 University of Wisconsin unites seventeen campuses.

1975 Menominee tribe regains federal recognition.

1987 State lottery is established.

1996 Wisconsin Works program is enacted.

Fast Facts

State capitol

Badger

Statehood date	May 29, 1848, the 30th state
Origin of state name	An Ojibwa word believed to mean "gathering of the waters"
State capital	Madison
State nickname	Badger State
State motto	"Forward"
State bird	Robin
State flower	Wood violet
State fish	Muskellunge
State rock	Red granite
State song	"On, Wisconsin!"
State tree	Sugar maple
State animal	Badger
State wildlife animal	White-tailed deer
State insect	Honeybee
State fossil	Trilobite
State grain	Corn
State dog	American water spaniel

Dairy cows

The Mississippi River
Valley

State domesticated animal	Dairy cow
State beverage	Milk
State mineral	Galena
State soil	Antigo silt loam
State fair	West Allis (early August)
Total area; rank	65,500 sq. mi. (105,412 sq km); 22nd
Land; rank	54,314 sq. mi. (87,410 sq km); 25th
Water; rank	11,186 sq. mi. (18,002 sq km); 3rd
***Inland water;* rank**	1,831 sq. mi. (2,947 sq km); 11th
***Great lakes;* rank**	9,355 sq. mi. (15,055 sq km); 2nd
Geographic center	Wood, 9 miles (14 km) southeast of Marshfield
Latitude and longitude	Wisconsin is located approximately between 42° 30' and 47° 3' N and 86° 49' and 92° 54' W.
Highest point	Timms Hill, 1,952 feet (595 m)
Lowest point	581 feet (177 m) along Lake Michigan
Largest city	Milwaukee
Number of counties	72
Longest river	Wisconsin River, 430 miles (692 km)
Population; rank	4,906,745 (1990 census); 16th
Density	87 persons per sq. mi. (34 per sq km)
Population distribution	66% urban, 34% rural

Wisconsin classroom

Cross-country skiing

Horicon National
Wildlife Refuge

Ethnic distribution (does not equal 100%)	White	92.25%
	African-American	5.00%
	Hispanic	1.91%
	Asian and Pacific Islanders	1.10%
	Other	0.85%
	Native American	0.81%

Record high temperature 114°F (46°C) at Wisconsin Dells on July 13, 1936

Record low temperature –54°F (–48°C) at Vanderbilt on January 24, 1922

Average July temperature 70°F (21°C)

Average January temperature 14°F (–10°C)

Average yearly precipitation 31 inches (79 cm)

Wisconsin's Natural Areas

National Lakeshores and Riverways

Apostle Islands National Lakeshore is comprised of islands and the Bayfield Peninsula on Lake Superior.

Saint Croix National Scenic Riverway contains 252 miles (406 km) of the Saint Croix and Namekagon rivers.

National Forests

Chequamegon National Forest is Wisconsin's largest national forest.

Nicolet National Forest, in northeastern Wisconsin, has more than 260 lakes.

**Apostle Islands
National Lakeshore**

National Scientific Reserve

Ice Age National Scientific Reserve includes a 1,000-mile (1,600-km) trail through scenery left by the Wisconsin glacier in nine state parks.

State Parks and Forests

Wisconsin has nine state forests, forty-seven state parks, fourteen state trails, and four recreation areas. The largest state forest, *North Highland-American Legion State Forest*, covers nearly 222,000 acres (89,000 ha) in northern Wisconsin. The largest state park is *Devil's Lake.*

Sports Teams

NCAA Teams (Division 1)

Marquette University Golden Eagles

University of Wisconsin-Green Bay Phoenix

University of Wisconsin-Madison Badgers

University of Wisconsin-Milwaukee Panthers

Major League Baseball

Milwaukee Brewers

National Basketball Association

Milwaukee Bucks

National Football League

Green Bay Packers

The Green Bay Packers

Ringling Theater in Baraboo

The Experimental Aircraft Association Museum

University of Wisconsin-Madison

Cultural Institutions

Libraries

Milwaukee Public Library is the leading public library in the state.

State Historical Society Library (Madison) contains extensive collections on state history.

Museums

State Historical Museum (Madison) contains extensive collections on Wisconsin history.

Circus World Museum (Baraboo) is located at the original site of the Ringling Brothers and Barnum & Bailey Circus winter headquarters.

Clown Hall of Fame (Milwaukee) honors clowns from around the world.

Milwaukee Public Museum is one of the largest natural history museums in the United States.

Rhinelander Logging Museum houses its exhibits in a replica of an old-time logging camp.

Experimental Aircraft Association Museum (Oshkosh) and *National Railroad Museum* (Green Bay) contain fine collections on air and rail equipment.

Performing Arts

Wisconsin has two major opera companies, one major symphony orchestra, and one major dance company.

Universities and Colleges

In the mid-1990s, Wisconsin had thirty public and thirty-four private institutions of higher learning.

Annual Events

January–March

Winterfest in Milwaukee (January)

World Championship Snowmobile Derby in Eagle River (January)

Hot Air Balloon Rally in Hudson (February)

American Birkebeiner in Cable and Hayward (February)

Milwaukee Sports Show (March)

April–June

Chocolate Festival in Burlington (May)

Great Wisconsin Dells Balloon Rally (June)

Walleye Weekend in Fond du Lac (June)

World Championship Off-Road Races in Crandon (June)

Asian Moon Festival in Milwaukee (June)

Polish Fest in Milwaukee (June)

Summerfest in Milwaukee (June)

July–September

Art Fair on the Square in Madison (July)

Great Circus Parade in Milwaukee (July)

Italian Fest in Milwaukee (July)

German Fest In Milwaukee (July)

Lumberjack World Championships in Hayward (July)

Experimental Aircraft Association Fly-In in Oshkosh (July)

Wisconsin State Fair in Milwaukee (August)

Africa Fest in Milwaukee (August)

Irish Fest in Milwaukee (August)

Mexican Fiesta in Milwaukee (August)

Summerfest in Milwaukee

The annual Mexican Fiesta

Cranberry bog

National Water Ski Show Championships in Janesville (August)

Cranberry Festival in Warrens (September)

Native American Fest in Milwaukee (September)

Oktoberfest in La Crosse (September–October)

October–December

Colorama, statewide (October)

Fall Flyway in the Great Horicon Marsh (October)

World Dairy Expo in Madison (October)

Holiday Folk Fair in Milwaukee (November)

Aldo Leopold

Golda Meir

Famous People

Walter Annenberg (1908–)	Media tycoon and philanthropist
Carrie Jacobs Bond (1862–1946)	Songwriter
Daniel C. Brandenstein (1943–)	Astronaut
Carrie Chapman Catt (1859–1947)	Social reformer
August Derleth (1909–1971)	Author
Edna Ferber (1885–1968)	Author
Zona Gale (1874–1938)	Author
King Camp Gillette (1855–1932)	Industrialist
Marguerite Henry (1902–1997)	Author
Woody Herman (1913–1987)	Jazz musician
Harry Houdini (1874–1926)	Magician and escape artist
Aldo Leopold (1887–1948)	Environmentalist
Jackie Mason (1931–)	Comedian
Joseph R. McCarthy (1908–1957)	Politician
Golda Meir (1898–1978)	Prime Minister of Israel

Laura Ingalls Wilder

Georgia O'Keeffe (1887–1986)	Artist
William Rehnquist Jr. (1924–)	Chief justice, U.S. Supreme Court
John Ringling (1866–1936)	Circus entrepreneur
Spencer Tracy (1900–1967)	Actor
Orson Welles (1915–1985)	Actor and director
Laura Ingalls Wilder (1867–1957)	Author
Thornton Wilder (1897–1975)	Playwright
Frank Lloyd Wright (1867–1959)	Architect

To Find Out More

History

- Aylesworth, Thomas G., and Virginia L. Aylesworth. *Western Great Lakes: Illinois, Iowa, Minnesota, Wisconsin*. New York: Chelsea House, 1995.

- Bratvold, Gretchen. *Wisconsin*. Minneapolis: Lerner Publications, 1991.

- Fradin, Dennis Brindell. *Wisconsin*. Chicago: Childrens Press, 1994.

- Krull, Kathleen, and David Hautzig (photographer). *One Nation, Many Tribes: How Kids Live in Milwaukee's Indian Community*. New York: Lodestar Books, 1995.

- Zeinert, Karen. *Wisconsin*. Tarrytown, N.Y.: Marshall Cavendish, 1997.

Biographies

- Anderson, Peter. *Aldo Leopold: American Ecologist*. New York: Franklin Watts, 1995.

- Anderson, William. *Laura Ingalls Wilder: A Biography*. New York: HarperCollins, 1995.

- Adler, David A. *Our Golda: The Story of Golda Meir*. New York: Viking Press, 1986.

Fiction

- Brink, Carol Ryrie. *Caddie Woodlawn*. New York: Simon & Schuster, 1983.

- Carter, Alden R. *Bull Catcher*. New York: Scholastic, 1997.

- Wilder, Laura Ingalls. *Little House in the Big Woods*. New York: Harper & Row, 1932.

Websites

- **State of Wisconsin Web Page**
  http://www.state.wi.us/
  The official state website for Wisconsin

- **Wisconsin Information and Websites**
  http://infomad.com/wisconsin
  Wide-ranging links to recreational, cultural, governmental, and media websites

- **Wisconsin Online**
  http://www.wistravel.com/
  Travel and tourism information for the state of Wisconsin

Addresses

- **Wisconsin Division of Tourism**
  123 West Washington Avenue
  P.O. Box 7970
  Madison, WI 53707
  For travel and tourism information about Wisconsin

- **Office of the Governor**
  State Capitol
  Box 7863
  Madison, WI 53707
  For information about the history of Wisconsin

Index

Page numbers in *italics* indicate illustrations.

Meet the Author

She may have physically left Wisconsin for many years, but since birth, Jean F. Blashfield has been a Wisconsinite. She returned to the state when she married and began to raise her own children.

Born in Madison, she lived on a farm in Middleton (now a busy suburb of the capital, without a farm in sight) when she started school. Her engineer-father's career took the family across the border into the Chicago area for most of her school years, but she promised she would return to Wisconsin someday.

During many years in publishing, she lived in Chicago, London, and Washington, D.C. But when she married Wallace Black (a Chicago publisher, writer, and pilot) and began to raise a family, she returned to Wisconsin. Today, she has two college-age children, three cats, and two computers in her Victorian home in Delavan.

Jean Blashfield has written about seventy-five books, most of them for young people. She likes best to write about interesting places, but she loves history and science, too. She has created an encyclopedia of aviation and space, written popular books on murderers and house plants, and had a lot of fun creating an early book on the things women have done, called *Hellraisers, Heroines, and Holy Women.*

She and Wally later formed their own company, which took advantage of Jean's massive collection of 3 x 5 cards. The cards contained interesting tidbits of information about many states, their places and people. Today, Jean Blashfield has all that research on computer. In fact, she uses computers to broaden her research on Wisconsin and many other subjects.

She says it's been a special joy to work on this book on Wisconsin. When writing a book for young people, she's often challenged as much by what to leave out of the book as by what to put in. This was especially true for the book on Wisconsin because she loves the state and its fascinating little corners and lively people so much.

Photo Credits

Photographs ©:

Allsport USA: 6 bottom, 125 (Vandystadt), 121, 131 bottom (Al Bello)
AP/Wide World Photos: 43, 92 top
Archive Photos: 7 bottom, 91 (Museum of the City of New York), 36, 134 bottom
Audrey Gibson: 79
Corbis-Bettmann: 81, 89, 101, 122
DNR Photo: 62, 109, 130 center, 133 top (Robert Queen)
Envision: 110 (Paul Poplis)
Greg Anderson: 90, 132 bottom
Library of Congress: 32
Mark E. Gibson: 6 top right, 39, 58, 66, 70, 75 top
National Geographic Image Collection: 16 (Kenneth Love)
North Wind Picture Archives: 17, 18, 20, 21, 23, 27, 30, 33
Robert Queen WI DNR: 76
State Historical Society of Wisconsin: 113
The Picture Cube: 19 (Nels Akerlund), 13, 15, 71 (Paul C. Butterbrodt), cover, 6 top center, 12, 55, 77, 96, 117, 129 top (Ken Dequaine), back cover (Dale Guldan), 29, 73, 80 (David A. Jentz), 108, 112 (Susan Lina Ruggles), 106 (Alan Magayne-Rosh), 78 (William Meyer), 72, 132 center (H. J. Morrill), 104, 2 (Eric Oxendorf), 24, 28, 41, 133 bottom (Susan Lina Ruggles), 9 (Ken Wardius), 7 top left, 38, 67, 94, 103 top (Scott J. Witte)
Tony Stone Images: 99 bottom, 118 bottom, 120, 132 top (Glen Allison), 53 (Tom Bean), 6 top left, 7 top center, 8, 50 (Ryan Beyer), 75 bottom (Sally Beyer), 129 bottom (Ryan Beyer), 34, 48, 130 top (Robert E. Daemmrich), 25, 59, 61, 99 top, 130 bottom, 134 top (Terry Donnelly), 107 (Hulton Getty), 51, 83 (Cathlyn Melloan), 87, 128 top (Peter Pearson), 47 (Scott Robinson), 7 top right, 98 (Michael Rosenfeld), 57, 131 top (Phil Schermeister), 65 (Don Smetzer), 92 center, 92 bottom, 128 bottom (Tom Tietz), 26, 88, 116 (Zane Williams)
University of Wisconsin-Madison Archives: 56, 134 center
UPI/Corbis-Bettmann: 103 bottom, 119, 135
UW-Madison News & Public Affairs: 82, 115, 124 (Jeff Miller)
UWE/Corbis: 40
Wisconsin Dept. of Natural Resources: 44, 46 (Stanley Sulliam), 52
Maps by XNR Productions, Inc.